COLLINS ANGLING

THE ART OF COARSE FISHING
WATER CRAFT

Introduction by John Bailey

CollinsWillow

An Imprint of HarperCollins*Publishers*

First published in 1993 by
Collins Willow
an imprint of HarperCollins Publishers
London

Based on The Art of Fishing
© Eaglemoss Publications Ltd 1993

A CIP catalogue record for this book is
available from the British Library

ISBN 0 00 218513 X

Printed and bound in Hong Kong

Contents

Introduction
Pages 7-8

1: Finding fish in still waters
Peaceful ponds • Small, deep pits • Park lakes
Winter lakes • Estate lakes • Summer reservoirs
Winter gravel pits • Boat-fishing lakes • Freshwater docks
Autumn still waters • Winter reservoirs
Pages 9-54

2: Finding fish in rivers
Fast, clear rivers • Lowland rivers • Small summer rivers
Large coloured rivers • A small fast winter river • Weirpools
River boatyards • Norfolk Broads in summer • Mill pools
Tidal rivers • Autumn rivers • Flooded rivers
Pages 55-104

3: Finding fish in canals and drains
Urban canals • Large relief drains • Fenland drains
Deep, wide canals • Winter fen drains
Pages 105-126

Index
Pages 127-128

Introduction

I was five years old, fishing on a northern canal, when a famous angler of the time, Albert Oldfield, told me not to worry about tackle, rigs and bait. "Find the fish first, lad," he said. "You'll do nowt till you do that." Every one of my 30-odd fishing seasons since, Albert has been proved right and I'm convinced that an angler without water craft is an angler without fish.

I know another thing: you can ask Graham Marsden, Nigel Witham, Jon Culley, Bill Rushmer, Neville Fickling, Roy Marlow, Mark Downes or any of the other experts who have contributed to this book and every one of them will agree with me that location is the key to successful angling. Baits, tackle and rigs are all vital but first you need to find your fish, by understanding their movements and their feeding habits.

In many ways, the consistently successful angler is like a nature detective. He will watch the swans feeding in the wintry shallows and know that some of the weed still lives on there, attracting small fish. The observant angler will watch a pair of grebes working an area around the mouth of a bay and know that it will be packed with food fish for perch or pike. Or he may watch where the prevailing winds strike the shore, realizing that a food store for roach and bream is being built up there which will attract shoals before long. He will recognize certain types of lilies and reeds and this will tell him the bottom make-up and even the depth of the water they grow in. Everything he sees will mean something to him, and piece by piece he will build up the whole jigsaw of a water.

▶

Successful water craft demands a great deal of thought and concentration if you are to read the signs accurately. Binoculars are very useful for zooming in on disturbed weedbeds or feeding fish. They may pick up the spiked dorsal fin of a perch as it tears into a shoal of tiny roach to take its meal, or even identify the backs of bream, far out in the choppy water over a gravel bar, before they go down to feed. Polaroid glasses are also invaluable, allowing you to see into the water and watch how tench tip and feed over a bed of particle baits or how a chub hunts a crayfish or engulfs a slug with total relish. For the angler who takes water craft seriously there are always new discoveries at the waterside and even the most humble pond reveals a changing and challenging environment to explore.

Albert Oldfield was wrong about one thing. He told me: "There's nowt to beat experience, lad." Well there is: this book. For me, it has been very rewarding to study carefully the detailed drawings of typical waters. By doing the same you will soon understand why the seasons have their effect, why the weather matters and why bottom contours, weed growth and snags are also significant. In fact, before long, you will be in touch with the very heartbeat of your own local waters and beginning to enjoy consistent success.

The scope of this book is immense: every type of still water, river, canal and drain is covered in this expert guide. You need never again have that gloomy, lost feeling of standing in front of a water and thinking, where on earth do I start? There is help right here, in one of the most valuable books I could possibly recommend to any coarse angler.

John Bailey

CHAPTER ONE

FINDING FISH
IN STILL WATERS

THE ART OF COARSE FISHING

WATER CRAFT

Peaceful ponds

Many anglers never give ponds a second look and so miss out on the chance of a peaceful day's fishing with some surprising rewards.

S mall, intimate waters where you can easily cast to the middle with light float tackle, ponds are regrettably not as plentiful in Britain as they once were. Urban sprawl and widespread land drainage have seen many of our ponds disappear forever. Enough ponds remain, however, to offer anglers prepared to search them out a relaxing change from larger, more heavily fished waters.

Likely candidates
Look for a pond that has both open and shaded water. Such a pond is likely to support a healthy balance of plants, insects and the fish that feed on them.

Avoid water surrounded by trees. Deep shade prevents the growth of plants that might harbour insects and this, in turn, means a lack of food for fish. Equally unpromising is a pond with no shade at all:

it may become choked with weed and, in hot weather, even dry up.

With the right mix of plant and insect life, you can find a surprising variety of fish. The most common species in ponds are probably rudd and tench, but you can also find roach, crucian carp, carp, bream, pike, perch and eels.

A mixed catch
Specimen fish are rare in ponds because the fish have to compete for a limited amount of food in a small volume of water. Where food is in very short supply, the fish are stunted. This is also the case when a pond has no pike or perch to cull the small fish and so becomes overcrowded. In a good pond, however, you can expect carp and pike to 7lb (3.2kg), tench and bream to 3lb (1.4g) and rudd, roach, crucian carp, perch and eels to 1lb (0.45kg).

▼ *Find a pond with a healthy balance of shaded and open water and you can expect to find a variety of water weeds, plenty of insect life – and a good head of fish.*

In any water supporting rudd, roach and bream, the species tend to interbreed but hybrids are especially common in ponds; cramped conditions allow for only one spawning area, so odd-looking offspring are inevitable.

Signs of life

Many promising ponds are ignored by anglers who don't take the trouble to study them for signs of life. Using binoculars, you can first study the water from a distance and spot any activity without disturbing the fish. Closer in, wear polarising glasses so that you can look through the surface glare to see what's below.

Look for signs of feeding fish. Reedmace stems swaying jerkily betray tench, carp or bream rooting between the stalks. Twitching lily pads indicate rudd picking water snails off the stems and undersides of the leaves. Cloudy patches or puffs of muddy water mean tench, carp or bream

are sifting the bottom silt for food. Small swirls or spreading rings on the surface give away rudd taking insects and other food items from below.

Feeding tench sometimes send up characteristic clusters of pinhead-sized bubbles. Larger bubbles may mean feeding carp or bream, or they may be pockets of gas escaping from the bottom mud. Watch carefully for a few minutes. If the bubbles keep on

Where to find the fish		
Fish	**Location**	**Techniques**
Rudd	Lilies, open water	Light waggler or pole
Tench, carp, bream	Close to weeds	Lift float; freelining
Roach, skimmer bream, perch	Open water	Light waggler or pole

▼ *Ponds are perfect places for getting away from it all – and the fishing can be great fun for the beginner and seasoned angler alike.*

Pondweeds and other plants oxygenate the water and harbour insects.

Overhanging trees shade the water, preventing weed from growing.

Water-lilies are good places to look for rudd picking snails off the undersides of the pads.

tench

rudd

roach

carp

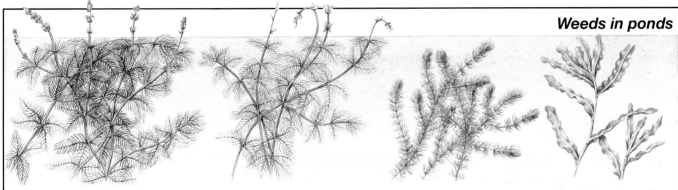

Weeds in ponds

Spiked water-milfoil (*Myriophyllum spicatum*) roots itself firmly in the mud at the bottom of ponds and slow streams all over Britain.

Alternate-flowered water-milfoil (*Myriophyllum alterniflorum*) is much rarer – it is found in peaty ponds.

Rigid hornwort (*Ceratophyllum demersum*) is common in England and Ireland, rare elsewhere.

Curled pondweed (*Potamogeton crispus*) grows in many ponds throughout Britain.

coming up from the same spot, they are probably gas, but if they come up from a slightly different spot each time they are almost certainly caused by fish.

Pond fishing

There are many enjoyable methods of fishing ponds – all using simple rigs and short casts that provide perfect relaxation for the seasoned angler and great practice for the beginner. Even the depth of the water can be estimated without too much trouble: just look at the plant life in and around the pond for some useful pointers.

In shallow margins you can expect to find reedmace and flowering rushes. As the water deepens, there may well be milfoils, hornworts, pondweeds and water-lilies. Only the deepest area is likely to be clear of weed.

Good baits for all pond fish are bread

▼ *Rudd are one of the most beautiful of all coarse fish and are abundant in ponds. Fish for them with lighly shotted float tackle.*

Seasonal habitats

Winter Pond fish tend to lie dormant in the deepest water in winter, using the pond bed with its weed roots as cover.
Spring As the water warms up in spring, the fish start to move into the shallow margins to spawn in the weedbeds.
Summer and autumn Fish seek the shade of weeds and lilies on hot, still summer days, moving into the margins from dusk to dawn to feed. On windy days in summer and autumn, you'll find most fish on the windward shore, where warm, oxygenated water, along with insects and other food, are driven.

paste, flake and crust, maggots, sweetcorn and worms. However, delicate tackle is the real key to success in pond work. Try small floats, and line and hooks in keeping with the size of fish you expect. Above all, learn to lose the traditional 'box-on-the-bank, sitting on top of the swim' approach. Wear camouflaged clothing and soft shoes so you won't be seen or heard by fish right at the water's edge. Get your tackle together well back from the bank and keep spare equipment in a shoulder bag to minimize your movements.

If the water is very shallow, freelining is a good method for tench, carp and bream. 'Cup' (mould) groundbait around the line above the hook with your hand to provide casting weight and attract the fish. This is a particularly good method on summer evenings when fish move into the margins to feed.

Fish the open water on-the-drop with a small, lightly shotted waggler or pole rig for rudd, roach, skimmer bream and perch. Feed little and often with samples of your hookbait and small balls of sloppy groundbait to attract the fish.

Another method is to fish on the bottom close to weeds for bottom-feeding tench, carp and larger bream. A simple lift-float rig is as good as any here.

Always go steady on the groundbait when fishing ponds, even if the fish are biting freely. It is easy to overestimate the number of fish and so overfeed them.

In late autumn and into winter, when the fish are less active and the water is usually much clearer, it is often best not to use any groundbait at all, sticking instead to sparing loosefeeding of your hookbait.

▶ *A pond completely surrounded by trees gets too little sunlight to support plant, insect and fish life and soon fills up with leaves.*

'Cupping' groundbait

When freelining, try 'cupping' or moulding groundbait around the line above the hook to provide casting weight and attract fish.

Fishing the lift-float

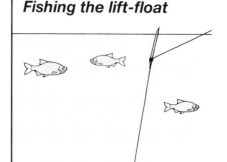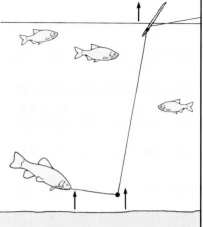

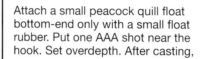

Attach a small peacock quill float bottom-end only with a small float rubber. Put one AAA shot near the hook. Set overdepth. After casting,

tighten up to sink the float to its tip. When a fish bites it takes the weight of the shot, causing the float to lift out of the water.

Finding the fish in small, deep pits

Down in the depths of small, deep pits lurk some monster carp and perch. How do you begin, when faced with a featureless hole? Deep thinking angler Graham Marsden has the answers...

S mall, deep pits can be natural or man-made. The natural ones are often found in rocky, boulder-strewn areas where deep fissures have flooded. Man-made ones are usually the flooded holes that remain after excavations of brick, slate, sand, gravel or any other quarrying.

◀ *Graham Marsden frequently fishes small, deep pits. This big carp is typical of the fish you can expect... with luck!*

▼ *Fishing deep pits in the winter is frequently more productive than fishing shallower still waters.*

There's quite a difference between these waters. Some may be simply a deep hole with no more character than a bucket; other excavations may have left a lake full of features. These can include steps, ledges, grooves and ridges, and deeper holes within holes.

Jobs in the pit

Finding and identifying the features should be your first job. All you need is a sliding float and a plummet. Walk around the pit, casting into as many areas as possible. In smaller pits you can plumb all areas without resorting to a boat, though it is still a time-consuming task to do properly.

It is important to plumb each feature thoroughly, so that you know exactly where the water begins to deepen; where it begins to shallow again; and the exact location of any grooves or bars.

At the same time, you can discover if there are any snags – such as sunken branches and rocks. Unfortunately, finding them might cost you your float and plummet, but it prevents losing the tackle *and* a fish later on!

With so few of the pit's natural features visible on the surface, finding out all you

can about what is happening below the surface becomes very important.

What's down there?

All the species of coarse fish normally found in still waters can be found in small, deep pits. However, the dominant species are usually carp and perch. These two generally grow to a good size where there is enough natural food to provide the necessary growth rate.

Other species may not grow so large. Bream and pike, in particular, require a larger water to reach specimen size.

Temperature layers

Anglers fishing such deep waters discover a number of interesting features. One is that, except in winter, the fish are unlikely to be feeding lower than 6m (20ft) down. In the warmer months the water below this level –

▶ **Deep pits are not the easiest of places to land fish. Get carried away wading in too far, and you might find yourself 12m (40ft) underwater! A telescopic landing net is an essential piece of equipment to save you having to wade into the pit.**

Big perch

For big perch a running paternoster and a size 6 hook work well in deep water. Allow the perch to take up to 1m (3ft) of line before striking, and don't play it to the net too quickly.

Perch can't adjust their swim bladders fast enough to cope with the change of water pressure when coming from the deeps; in some cases the swim bladder protrudes into the mouth. However, if you allow them a rest in a carp sack, they usually survive and can be put back.

at about 4°C (39.2°F) – is too cold for the fish.

At a depth of about 6m (20ft) there is a band of water that changes temperature rapidly. This is called the thermocline. In summer the water above this band is warm – this encourages fish such as carp to head for the surface. However, in the depths of winter this upper layer may be considerably colder than the lower level – which remains at a steady 4°C (39.2°F).

Characterful areas

In small waters there is no one particular spot where fish can be found. They are usually wanderers, rooting for food in all areas. However, they still have their favourite haunts, and for many fish these are the 'shallows' (which may be as deep as 3m/10ft

Pondweed indicates shallow margins, but don't be tempted to wade.

Bushes and grasses around the edge of the pit show it is a mature water.
Newly established waters are frequently quite bare around the bank.

DOWN IN THE DEEP DARK PIT

anyway) and where any weed – such as amphibious bistort – is likely to grow.

The deeper water, which can be over 12m (40ft) deep in some small pits, is home to perch in particular, and to many other species in winter when the surface water has dropped below the significant 4°C (39.2°F). The lower level of water in pits – that below about 6m (20ft) – is unlikely to fall below this temperature except when a strong wind causes the water layers to tilt.

Small jack pike lurk behind rushes for passing fish.

Very steep sides are a feature of old mines, brick pits and tin workings. Be very careful and never wade.

Tilting temperature layers

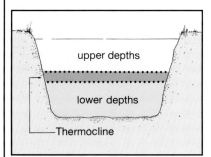
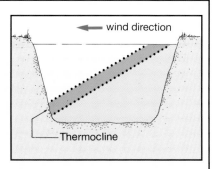

The water below 6m (20ft) remains at a constant 4°C (39.2°F). In summer this is the cooler layer, in winter it is the warmer. Strong winds can tilt the layers, which affects the distribution of fish.

When this happens the cold water is pushed on to one side and the warm water on the other.

The areas with character are always worth investigating. These could be the base of a drop-off, the bottom of a groove, the peak of a bar – in fact anywhere that can grow or trap food, offer security from preda-

▶ Small pits can often contain some very big perch. Try fishing for them with a running paternoster, using lobworms and minnows as bait. Your reward may well be just such a fine specimen as this one.

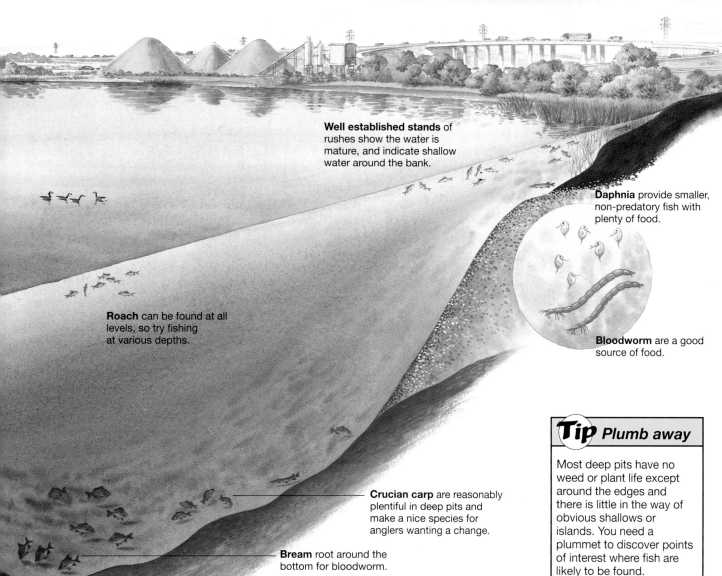

Well established stands of rushes show the water is mature, and indicate shallow water around the bank.

Daphnia provide smaller, non-predatory fish with plenty of food.

Roach can be found at all levels, so try fishing at various depths.

Bloodworm are a good source of food.

Crucian carp are reasonably plentiful in deep pits and make a nice species for anglers wanting a change.

Bream root around the bottom for bloodworm.

Tip Plumb away

Most deep pits have no weed or plant life except around the edges and there is little in the way of obvious shallows or islands. You need a plummet to discover points of interest where fish are likely to be found.

In the swim

A particular problem with all deep pits is that the banks can drop away very steeply – you may have great difficulty getting out if you fall in. There could also be underwater snags to trap you.

It pays to wear a life jacket if you can't swim. It's wisest to fish these places with another person who can go for help in case of difficulties.

► *A typical small deep pit. This one, near Graham's home at Stoke-on-Trent, shows some characteristic features – or rather lack of surface features.*

tors, or provide an ambushing spot from which predators can hunt.

Tactics for the deep

On some small, deep pits carp love roving the water with their backs protruding, or at least close enough to the surface to cause bow waves.

Every now and again one disappears, only for a mass of tiny bubbles to explode on the surface as the carp dives to the bottom to root for bloodworm or some other succulent morsel. The key to catching them lies in using the bait that is most obvious in deep water. At such depths sight may well be less important than smell.

To catch them, use an oily bait. Try boilies soaked in fish oils, or one of the oils sold specially for boilie soaks. Tinned meatballs are another successful bait in such deep waters. These are very oily, and are best steeped in greasy gravy, perhaps mixed with a little groundbait. Use either a whole one, or half on a hook.

When you throw in a few samples of meatballs – or any other very greasy bait – an oil slick forms on the surface. The bait also leaves an oily trail through the water as it sinks. It is a heart-stopping moment when you see a carp swim into an oil slick and immediately dive to follow the oily trail to its source.

A useful little trick is to watch for carp approaching and cast just before they actually enter the area. This way the oil trail from the bait is at its freshest and easiest to follow. Any of the usual legering methods – such as fishing link legers or bolt rigs with hair-rigged bait – are successful.

◄ *Carp love the deeper pits; in the winter they can root about in the depths, and in summer bask near the surface. Under such favourable conditions they can grow big.*

Park lakes

There's more to park lake fishing than children with small nets scooping out sticklebacks, says Les Hammond.

For years the quality of park lake fishing was one of the best kept secrets in angling but now the cat is well and truly out of the bag. Once dismissed by all but the few in the know, park lakes now attract anglers of all ages and abilities, from children to pensioners, from beginners to old hands.

One reason for their growing popularity is their accessibility. With transport increasingly expensive, more anglers are looking for good fishing close to home – and park lakes fit the bill.

Park lake potential

Most towns and cities have park lakes where you can fish for free or for the cost of a day ticket. Where you have to buy a day ticket there are often reduced rates for children, pensioners and the disabled.

The commonest fish in park lakes are roach, bream, carp, tench, perch and pike. Specimens are rare, as you might expect, but they can still grow to respectable sizes: bream and tench to 3lb (1.4kg), roach and perch to 1lb (0.45kg) and carp and pike to 10lb (4.5kg).

Like most shallow still-waters, park lakes tend to fish best in summer. If your picture of a park lake in summer is one of crowds and noise, don't despair. The only

▲ *Roach are the mainstay of sport on many park lakes. Use fine float tackle with very light shotting down the line to put together a good bag of these popular fish.*

▼ *There are many park lakes around the country offering good, cheap and – above all – easily accessible fishing. They are the ideal training grounds for young anglers.*

▲ Not all park lakes are small concrete bowls. Some are large, natural waters that let you forget you're close to the centre of town.

times parks are really too crowded for fishing in summer are in the middle of the day on hot weekends and public holidays.

Don't write off park lakes completely in winter. Obviously, you can't expect to bag up after a hard frost but pick a mild day and you can expect a worthwhile catch.

Reading the water

There's no such thing as a typical park lake. Some are shaped like a piece from a jigsaw puzzle and are little more than ponds. Others are just like large bowls.

One thing most park lakes have in common, however, is a lack of depth. Most are man-made and were built with boating safety in mind – shallow water ensures that the worst a boater is likely to suffer in an accident is a soaking. Therefore you seldom find more than 1m (3ft) of water anywhere.

When it comes to spotting fish-holding areas, park lakes differ from most other types of water in that obvious features are rare. Even those few spots that look good by all the usual rules of water craft don't necessarily hold fish.

There's usually very little weed, especially where there are lots of water birds and boats. When you do find interesting looking weed beds or lily pads it's likely that the water they're in is too shallow for fish.

Popular park lakes

The following are just a few of the many park lakes around the country where you can find good fishing, says Les Hammond.

● **Calderstones Park, Liverpool** Carp, tench, roach and pike. Free fishing.

● **Crooks Valley Park, Crooks, Sheffield** Good head of carp, tench, bream and roach. Day ticket on bank.

● **Danson Park, Bexleyheath, Kent** Big head of roach, plus some carp, perch and tench. Day ticket on bank.

● **Highgate Ponds, Hampstead Heath, North London** Roach, tench and bream with some carp, perch and pike. Free fishing.

● **Newsham Park, Liverpool** Carp, bream, tench and roach. Free fishing.

● **Princes Park, Liverpool** Mainly bream, tench and roach. Free fishing.

● **Salford Park, Salford, Manchester** Mainly roach and bream. Day ticket on bank.

● **Sefton Park, Liverpool** Carp, tench, roach and perch. Free fishing.

● **Victoria Park, Hackney, East London** Mostly roach and tench, with some carp and perch. Day ticket on bank.

● **Wanstead Park, Wanstead, East London** Roach, bream, tench, carp and pike. Day ticket on bank.

● **Wollerton Park, Wollerton, Nottingham** Good pike, plus tench, bream and roach. Day ticket on bank.

SUMMER IN THE PARK

Model boat enthusiasts and other park users have as much right to use the lake as anglers – so it is share and share alike!

The same goes for any trees hanging invitingly down to the water.

The margins of islands in any lake are always worth investigating for cruising carp but again there isn't always the necessary depth in park lakes.

So how do you find the fish? First, don't forget the obvious; park lakes are usually heavily fished and simply by watching and talking to other anglers you can quickly find out which are the best places to fish. If, by chance, there's no-one fishing then walk around the lake looking for fish topping or even bubbling. If there are no signs of any fish, then choose a spot where the wind – however slight – is in your face, not at your back. This is a good rule on most still waters because the wind blows food and warm surface water inshore.

Having picked your swim, how far out should you fish? At dawn and dusk, when the park is deserted, many fish lose their natural caution and move right into the margins to feed. During the day, when people are about, most fish tend to keep away from the banks. And the shallower the water, the farther out they stay.

Some park lakes are of uniform depth. Plumb carefully, however, and you often find very slight depressions. The silt tends to be thickest in such spots, making them

▲ *This young angler is trying the leger but light float tackle with regular loose feeding usually catches better on most park lakes.*

likely places to find tench, carp and bream rooting for bloodworm. If you find no such depression, fish as far out from the bank as you can comfortably cast and feed.

Other park lakes have very shallow margins, with the bottom sloping away gently then levelling out some way from the bank.

Public places

Parks are public places open to everyone, not just anglers. Remember, all have a right to use parks and when you fish park lakes you are in the public gaze. So arrange your tackle tidily out of the way of passers-by, and pick up any litter or line you see lying around before you start fishing.

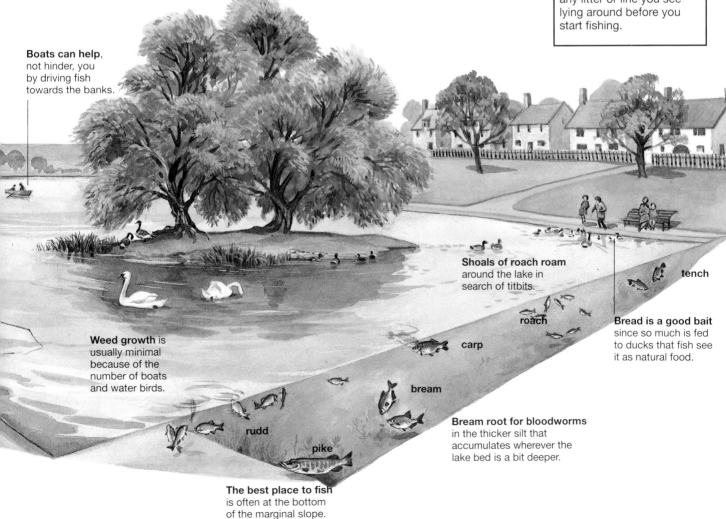

Boats can help, not hinder, you by driving fish towards the banks.

Shoals of roach roam around the lake in search of titbits.

tench

roach

Bread is a good bait since so much is fed to ducks that fish see it as natural food.

Weed growth is usually minimal because of the number of boats and water birds.

carp

bream

rudd

pike

Bream root for bloodworms in the thicker silt that accumulates wherever the lake bed is a bit deeper.

The best place to fish is often at the bottom of the marginal slope.

▲ *An angler reaches for his landing net as he gets the better of a park lake tench. The pole is a good method where you have a reasonable depth of water close in to the bank, but on many park lakes you need to use a waggler to reach the fish.*

▶ *Park lake fish can grow to surprisingly good sizes, as this plump tench shows. Such fish are great fun on light tackle and, since park lakes are usually free of snags, aren't hard to land if your tackle is balanced and your knots are properly tied.*

Boating bonus

Boats are the bane of anglers on many types of water but not on shallow park lakes. If they keep a reasonable distance out from the bank – as they usually do – boats can help by driving fish within casting range.

As for model boat enthusiasts, they're a mild mannered bunch in the main and tend to frequent very shallow bays – areas of little interest to the angler anyway.

Plumb carefully to find this point (it's often marked by a slight but definite drop-off) as it is a natural food trap.

Tackling park lakes

You don't need any special tackle, techniques or baits to fish park lakes.

Big fish such as pike and carp respond to any of the usual baits and methods. Bread often works just as well as boilies for carp, and can also be a good bait for the bigger bream, roach and tench. It's especially good where people regularly feed it to the ducks, but be warned – those same ducks can show more interest than the fish!

For a mixed bag of fish of all sizes, maggots and casters are a better bet. In summer it's usually best to feed hemp and caster and fish caster on the hook – maggots tend to attract too many small fish. In winter, when small fish are less of a problem, a lively maggot usually outfishes a static caster.

If you have deep enough water close in and there aren't too many people about, the pole can score, but usually you need a rod and reel to reach the fish. Legering works, but the waggler is nearly always the best method, especially in summer when you are mainly looking for bites on the drop.

Park lakes are usually hard fished so use fine tackle: size 18-24 hooks and hook-lengths of no more than 1½lb (0.68kg).

Use a straight waggler with a fine insert, and set the hook about 30cm (1ft) overdepth. Down the line you need only very light, evenly spread shotting – three or four no.10s at most. This allows your bait to fall slowly through the water. If you don't get a bite on the drop, try twitching the hookbait along the bottom.

Little and often

Because park lakes are usually so shallow and featureless, the fish tend to be nomadic, roaming around in search of food. You may therefore have to wait a while for your first bite, but by feeding little and often you can stop fish when they move into your swim. After a succession of bites your swim often dies as the fish wander off, but keep feeding and you'll stop them again the next time they come along.

Lakes in winter

Oxford angler Bruce Vaughan explains how preparation, observation and lakeside logic help you spot signs of activity and winkle out fish from their wintry homes.

As temperatures begin to fall with the onset of winter, stillwater fish tend to feed less (their metabolism slows down) and they become more localized.

Time spent on checking the water is never wasted – old advice it may be, but it's particularly relevant when lake fishing in winter. Finding the holding areas and feeding times is vital for success.

Shorten the odds

You can improve your chances of catching in a number of ways. The aim is to find the most likely spots and get your bait to the right place at the right time – where fish gather to feed.

Frequent fishing Fish a water, particularly one new to you, as often as possible and keep on switching swims until you find fish. The idea is not only to locate fish but to discover their feeding times – it's no use fishing all morning if the fish are late afternoon feeders. You can sometimes save time by asking local anglers where and when the fish feed.

Observation A vital part of the 'swim hopping' approach is to keep a constant watch on the water for signs of fish activity. Good

▼ *A semi-frozen scene – deep swims tend to be more productive in winter but fish move into shallow water warmed by a bright sun.*

Tip *Get your skates on*

On its day spinning can be a fun and fruitful pike puller. If you go on a spinning spree, stick to light gear so you can get around easily. You just need a rod, a landing net and a small shoulder bag or rucksack to carry spare lures, baits, traces and bits and pieces. Keep on the move, stopping to fish every characterful point.

On a sunny day, if the pike are active and hungry, lures may tempt them. But a deadbait might be better for torpid fish lounging on the bottom.

▼ *Fishing from a boat increases your chances by opening routes into awkward places. If you're lucky you might coax a fine perch like this 1½-pounder (0.7kg) out of the snags.*

Where there's one pike you'll usually find more nearby.

Pike and perch often inhabit the same zones of the lake.

WINTER LAKE SCENE

The water sometimes shallows up over raised parts of the lake bottom – a feature that often draws fish.

concentration and a keen eye are essential, since some of the visual clues are subtle. A big carp, for example, can break the surface and roll quite silently, with only the slightest ripple.

Main targets

Anything could turn up to surprise you in lakes during the cold season, but there are a few trusty species you can expect to show regularly – particularly in the deeper, warmer water.

Pike are probably the most sought-after species on winter lakes. You can see them striking at the surface when chasing or taking prey. Cast a bait directly at a swirl and you'll often get an instant take.

On many lakes pike grow up to a good size and are generally not too difficult to catch. Most big pike fall to deadbaits fished static, but there are more interesting ways to catch them – and a chance of netting a specimen too.

Spinning with artificial lures or small deadbaits is an enjoyable way of catching pike. A mobile approach is the order of the day, so take the minimum of gear.

Look for deep areas associated with islands, snaggy areas (flooded or fallen trees), gullies, weedbeds, overhanging trees and at the bottom of drop-offs. Pike like such places because they are frequented by the fish on which they feed. Baitfish gather in shoals during the winter months – attracted to these features because they

pike

perch

pike

carp

roach

carp

Carp patrol the margins and are regularly found in areas which were summer hotspots.

Roach shoals seek higher temperatures in deeper water during the winter months.

Perch live in shoals and use the cover of weedbeds, trees and other snags for ambushing their prey.

Pike hunt in snaggy areas, around submerged trees, islands and in the shallows.

provide a place of refuge and normally also a source of food.

You tend to find pike in concentrations rather than spread evenly throughout a lake. When you locate such a hotspot, give the spinner a try, but have a go with floatfished or legered deadbaits too.

Perch Features which are good holding spots for pike also attract another predatory species – the perch. They too are catchable with artificial lures or deadbaits, with the bait scaled down to suit the species.

It's worth bearing in mind the perch's marked preference for freshwater fish over salt water species when it comes to deadbaits. Perch live in shoals – so if you catch one there will be others nearby.

Fishing afloat

A really enjoyable way to spin or wobble deadbaits on a lake is to get afloat in a rowing boat. This way you can probe thoroughly the dense beds of reeds or rushes along the margins, which might be difficult to cover from the bank. Islands and plateaus are also more easily covered by boat anglers.

Trolling for pike is effective too. Suspend a deadbait under a float and tow it behind a

boat. Don't use more than two rods or you may get into a tangle.

If you can't get afloat in search of pike, you can still fish a bait at a distance using a vaned float. These catch the wind and can carry a bait a considerable way out into a lake – within the reach of more fish.

▼ *Make sure you wrap up warm enough for comfort – and don't forget the flask. You can have fine days too in the cold season but be prepared for any sudden changes in conditions.*

as underwater shelves and ledges, holes and the sites of weedbeds which die back in the winter.

Roach like to roll during periods of low light – their activity at these times is often a prelude to feeding. The best way to spot roach rolling is to walk along the banks of a lake at dawn or dusk.

Fish for roach facing into the wind when it's blowing strongly from a warm quarter (south or south-westerly in winter) and it could pay dividends – particularly where deep water is within casting range.

Choose from bread, sweetcorn, maggots and casters for bait. Leger or float fish these baits for best presentation according to conditions and casting range.

At this time of year you often find carp in places which were hotspots during the summer as long as there is depth. So it's usually more productive to fish in these areas rather than to try to entice fish to move into and feed in an area they don't normally frequent. If the water is warmed after a couple of sunny days carp may be drawn to shallower parts.

Keep your eyes peeled for signs of carp and remember that they love to patrol the margins but only do so if there is not too much bankside disturbance. They also root around in the dead lilies, weed and reedbeds and snaggy areas such as fallen trees.

▲ *Lure casting for pike on a clear winter's day. Try deadbaits if fishing with lures fails to catch any fish – pike unwilling to chase baits may be receptive to static offerings.*

Other takers

As the water gets colder, roach shoals seek the higher temperatures in deep water. The shoals continue to roam as they did during the summer and autumn months, but less widely. They also have a habit of returning frequently to favourable areas – such places

A prime pair of winter roach – just the sort of prize on offer if you make the effort and brave the elements.

Estate lakes

The great landscaped estates of the 18th century often featured lakes in their design. Some of these waters, accessible today, demand a carefully considered approach to water craft if you are to make the best of the hot spots, says John Bailey.

Many lakes were built in the grounds of great houses during the 18th century vogue for landscaping parklands. Most were formed by damming a stream or spring in a valley overlooked by the house.

Now around two hundred years old, some estate lakes are open to the general public for fishing on a day ticket basis – offering pleasant and challenging sport for anglers. Most still show signs of their original construction – important for the angler planning his fishing strategy. The lakes are often set in beautiful country surroundings and fine specimens can be taken from them. But they are difficult waters to fish and set a stern test of water craft skills.

▶ *Koi carp are found in some estate lakes, although they take a bit of catching. Their behaviour is typical of the other members of the carp family, but they seem to be a particularly shy and elusive fish.*

To land a fish like this fine one is quite a feat.

Special features

The dam end of the lake usually holds the deepest water, generally 1.5 to 4.5m (5ft to 15ft) deep. The lake gradually shelves from the deep end towards the shallows, where the water can virtually dry up in the course of a long, hot summer.

▼ *Day ticket fishing is available at some estate waters. You can relax in beautiful surroundings like these at Blenheim Palace, and you stand a good chance of catching fish as well.*

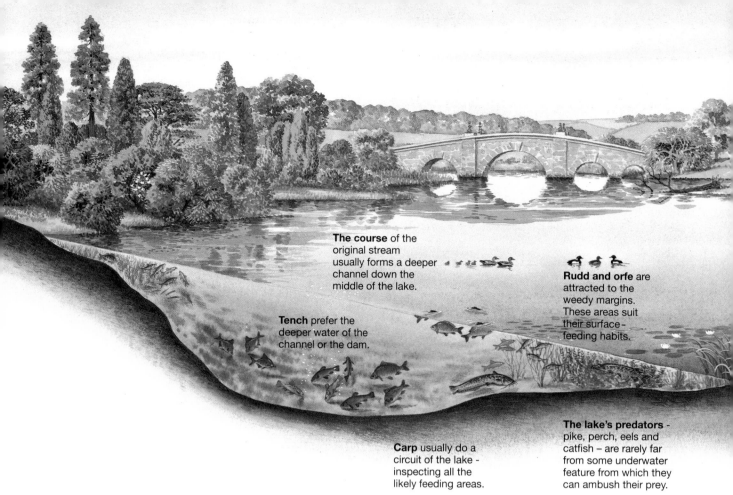

The course of the original stream usually forms a deeper channel down the middle of the lake.

Rudd and orfe are attracted to the weedy margins. These areas suit their surface-feeding habits.

Tench prefer the deeper water of the channel or the dam.

The lake's predators - pike, perch, eels and catfish – are rarely far from some underwater feature from which they can ambush their prey.

Carp usually do a circuit of the lake - inspecting all the likely feeding areas.

ESTATE LAKES – EXOTIC FISH

Frequently the lake holds a deep central channel marking the course of the original stream. Although often only a trickle, it can become quite active after a summer storm.

Remains of the original ornamentation can sometimes still be seen – these include islands and parts of boathouses or landing stages.

Vision and vegetation

The springs keep the water clear, but the lakes can cloud up if there are high fish stocks, dense populations of wildfowl or rich algal growths.

Luxuriant weed is unusual, but there can be extensive silting as a result of decades of leaves falling into the water – and never being removed. Large reed beds encroach around the margins and in the shallows, where the silting is most evident.

What to expect

The species of fish present reflect the lake's history. Some fish were introduced because they were considered good for the table, so you'll find plenty of tench and bream. Rudd are often present because they were a very common species 200 years ago. Carp were

◀ A splendidly marked golden tench – just one of the many species of fish held in the old waters of estate lakes.

Tench, once considered good eating, were highly prized by 18th century palates. Golden tench were introduced in the 19th century, along with various other imported species.

Wooded islands – with trees and bushes overhanging the water – provide extra food and shelter for many species.

Big perch can often be found around boathouses and landing stages.

Silty margins encourage the growth of large reed beds.

▶ *Looking every inch a country squire in a time warp, John Wilson – surrounded by 20th century tackle – plays a fish as anglers might have done 200 years ago.*

popular then as now – the original fish stocks were fully scaled commons. Mirror carp in estate lakes were introduced after World War II.

Pike, perch and eels may have stocked themselves – probably by entering through the original feeder streams. But other species present were certainly introduced during the late 19th century, when there was a great interest in natural history and a taste for introducing exotic species of plants and animals. Catfish, golden tench and orfe, often from Germany, are frequently found in estate lakes – survivors of the period.

Where to fish an estate lake

▶ *Claydon Lake, controlled by Leighton Buzzard Angling Club, is set in rural Buckinghamshire. It holds some big carp and catfish.*

Annual membership is available from local tackle shops and you also need an Anglian region rod licence.

Many estate lakes are privately owned, available only to members or by invitation, but some are open to the general public. Here are a few open on a day or season ticket basis. Phone for details of fees, opening times, conditions etc.
● **Blenheim Lake,** Oxfordshire Available for boat fishing

(Tel. 0993 811432).
● **Castle Howard Great North Lake,** Yorkshire (Tel. 0653 84331).
● **Clumber Park Lake,** Notts NT property (Tel. 0909 476592).
● **Nostell Priory Lakes,** Yorkshire (Tel. 0924 863562).
● **Gunton Park Lake,** Norfolk (Tel. 0502 730288).

Likely spots

Estate lakes can be anything from two to twenty acres in area. Their small size means fish can potentially be found in most parts of the lake. Nevertheless, different species favour distinct areas.

Tench prefer the deeper water along the dam and out in the central channel. But they feed happily in only 60cm (2ft) of water if the old bed is showing through the silt. They are also found in the shallows when spawning, so don't fish for them at this time. They shun the shallows, however, once the sun gets high and hot, or if there is a cold wind.

Carp often use the same areas as tench but they are fond of the sun, basking in the shallows on hot afternoons. They are also great travellers and can make a tour of the whole lake between dusk and dawn. They search for food everywhere, investigating lily

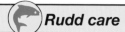
Rudd care

Rudd suffer particularly if subjected to bad handling.

To preserve small and fragile populations, make sure you return them straight away instead of keeping them in nets for long periods.

stems, fallen trees, exposed roots, boathouse brickwork and the rotting timbers of old landing stages. Their most favoured feeding areas are where the bottom is kept clear of mud and silt by springs or wind action.

Bream are roving fish and keep well away from the bank. They enjoy feeding in exposed areas of the lake where the wind whips up a bit of a ripple. You can spot them by the clouds of silt stirred up as they go down to feed.

▲ *All in a row – a line of matchmen at their pegs on the Great Water, Gunton, Norfolk.*
Fishing matches can be one way to get on to waters not otherwise open to the public.

◄*If there are catfish in the lake and you like a good fight, it is worth trying for them. A good bait is a matchbox-sized piece of squid on a size 2 hook.*

Rudd, even more wary than bream, are found in the thickest weed beds, in impenetrable bays or deep among the lilies.

Predatory fish such as pike, perch, eels and catfish make use of underwater ambush points in the lake. Islands, fallen trees, sunken boats, boathouse structures and the thickest weed beds generally harbour at least one predator.

Careful techniques

Approach the estate lake's clear waters carefully, using the most delicate gear within reason. As a guideline use a fairly powerful float rod and no less than 3-4lb (1.4-1.8kg) line for tench, and 2-3lb (0.9-1.4kg) for bream. For carp you need a carp rod and 6-7lb (2.7-3.2kg) line.

These lakes are ideal for surface fishing and their shallow, warm waters encourage carp, rudd and even tench to feed off the top.

Natural baits seem to do the trick. A large, lively lobworm on a size 4 or 6 hook is hard to beat for most species present.

Freeline or float fish the lobworm in all the likely, snag-ridden areas. A small portion of the large, freshwater swan mussel can also be used – if you can find any.

Particle baits work extremely well in old waters like these. Corn, maggots, casters, hempseed and nuts are all fine choices.

Ideally you should have a pre-baiting programme. It may not be possible to put in three to four pints every day for a week before fishing. But if you can introduce some of your particles beforehand, the better your chances of catching will be.

Reservoirs in summer

At first sight a reservoir may not seem the most exciting place to look for fish – but to the experienced angler the signs are there that point the way to large catches and big fish.

▼ *The valve (draw-off) tower attracts small fish, which in turn draw the predators. Here two anglers troll round the tower rather than fish the precarious dam wall.*

Reservoirs are man-made lakes constructed either to hold supplies of drinking water or to maintain the levels of canals during dry spells in the summer. A reservoir matures slowly after it has been filled with water, gradually becoming colonized by plant and animal species. Natural stocks of coarse fish from the feeder rivers then exploit these resources. As with many other types of fishery, it is becoming increasingly common to stock carp in reservoirs; they grow quickly, fight hard and so are popular with anglers.

There are two different types of reservoir: the concrete bowl and the flooded valley type. Flooded valleys are generally more scenic and pleasant to fish, though there is usually no difference in the quality of the

Top reservoirs

● **College Reservoir, near Falmouth, Cornwall** A 38 acre water, known for specimen carp, but there are large perch, bream and tench too. Day tickets from machines on the bank.
● **Denton Reservoir, Denton, Lincs.** An excellent all round fishery with carp, tench, roach, perch, bream and pike. Permits from the local tackle shop.
● **Naseby Reservoir, Northants.** An 85 acre water with good carp, tench and rudd. Season tickets from BWB, Willow Grange, Church Road, Watford WD1 3QA.
● **Staunton Harold Reservoir, near Melbourne, Derbyshire.** A popular 200 acre water with large shoals of bream, roach, tench and pike to over 25lb (11.3kg). Permits from Melbourne Gun and Tackle, High Street.
● **Sywell Reservoir, near Northampton** A large water best known for big tench. It also contains pike over 20lb (9.1kg), perch and roach. Permits from the local tackle shop.
● **Tring Reservoir, Herts.** This consists of three coarse fisheries – Wilstone, Startops and Marsworth. A specimen hunter's dream, these reservoirs have produced huge bream, roach, pike and tench. Permits available on the bank or from the bailiff. Night fishing is permitted for season ticket holders only.
● **Welford Reservoir, near Welford, Leics.** A 20 acre fishery with many specimen bream, carp, tench, pike, roach and rudd. Season tickets from BWB (address above).

Tactics for reservoir fishing

Species	Location	Best techniques
Bream	Deeper water, especially in open water or along the old course of the brook.	Legering or swimfeedering with maggot or worm.
Carp	Almost anywhere from shallows to the deeps. They like to patrol margins and around lily beds.	Legering sweetcorn or boilie, or floater fishing with crust.
Pike	Shallows in warmer weather. They like inlets or the valve tower or wherever there are fry.	Spoons, spinners and plugs, or sink and draw deadbait.
Perch	Deeper water, in bays, reedy areas and close to snags such as sunken bushes.	Small spoons and spinners, or legering lobworm or fish.
Roach	Deeper water, near the dam wall or in open water.	Floatfishing maggots or swimfeedering maggot, worm or bread.
Rudd	Shallows, especially in bays and around reeds or lilies.	Floatfishing maggot or bread on the drop.
Tench	Shallows, especially around weedbeds and lilies.	Floatfishing on the bottom or swimfeedering maggot, bread, worm, sweetcorn or paste.

fishing. At first the huge open expanses of water that make up these fisheries can be daunting, but with a little thought and effort, you can find the fish and have some fabulous sport.

Fair but featureless

Reservoirs do not usually have many visible features, but if the following are present, they can provide clues to the location of the fish.

Weedbeds, if they are present, attract all species of fish, especially tench in the shallow water at the margins and around any islands. These fish spawn in shallow weedy areas early in the season. The sport can be exceptional just after this, while they are feeding up to replace the energy and protein used up in the breeding process.

Valve towers and stream inlets – usually rich sources of food, shelter and oxygenated water – attract and hold a variety of small fish and fry. The presence of so many small fish draws the predators – pike and perch.

Old valley features, such as hedgerows, fences, roads, trees and the remains of buildings which became submerged when the valley was flooded to create the reservoir, also

A FLOODED VALLEY RESERVOIR IN SUMMER

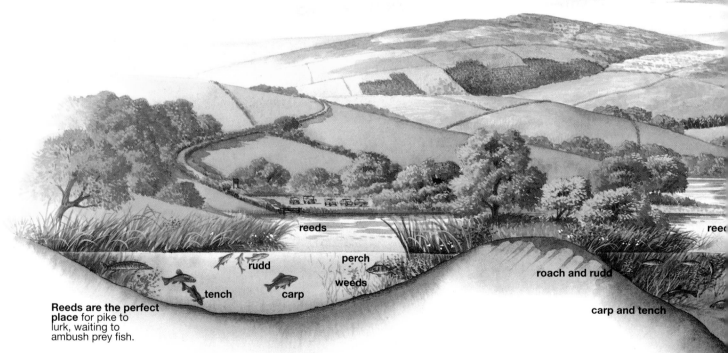

reeds

rudd

perch

weeds

tench

carp

roach and rudd

reed

carp and tench

Reeds are the perfect place for pike to lurk, waiting to ambush prey fish.

▶ *Carp like this 17lb (7.7kg) common are a highly popular reservoir quarry. In the generally snag-free waters carp can run and take to the depths when hooked, which makes for an exciting struggle. In summer, carp are often caught right under the rod tip in the margins.*

hold many fish. These are best located using an old map of the area, though sometimes asking other anglers can be fruitful. In the absence of either of these two sources of information, try working your way round the reservoir with a plummet – seeking out snaggy or uneven areas.

The original course of the stream is another feature found on old maps. If it is within casting distance, it can produce big catches of the bream which patrol along it regularly, searching for food.

◄ *Water levels can be greatly reduced in summer, making some marginal areas too shallow to be worth fishing, but opening up new swims to the bank fisherman. Here, Burrator Reservoir near Plymouth is visibly about 1.5m (5ft) down. A run of dry summers can prevent some waters from being full at any time of year.*

Tip **First time**

On your first few trips to a particular reservoir, choose a fishing position – such as a peninsula – which gives you a good view of the rest of the water. From your vantage point you should have a good view of any fish rolling or topping and where the anglers are catching fish.

The dam wall is often a productive spot since you can reach deep water easily. Any food particles drifting over to it become trapped at the bottom of the wall.

Fish activity – greatest at dawn and dusk – is the best way to locate most species of fish. Simply walk round the water armed with binoculars, looking for fish rolling and topping and, in the case of the bottom feeders, bubbles and clouds of coloured water. Activity, both on the bottom and at the surface, can indicate feeding fish.

Using the weather

Though each species of fish prefers to live in certain areas of a water (bream, roach, perch

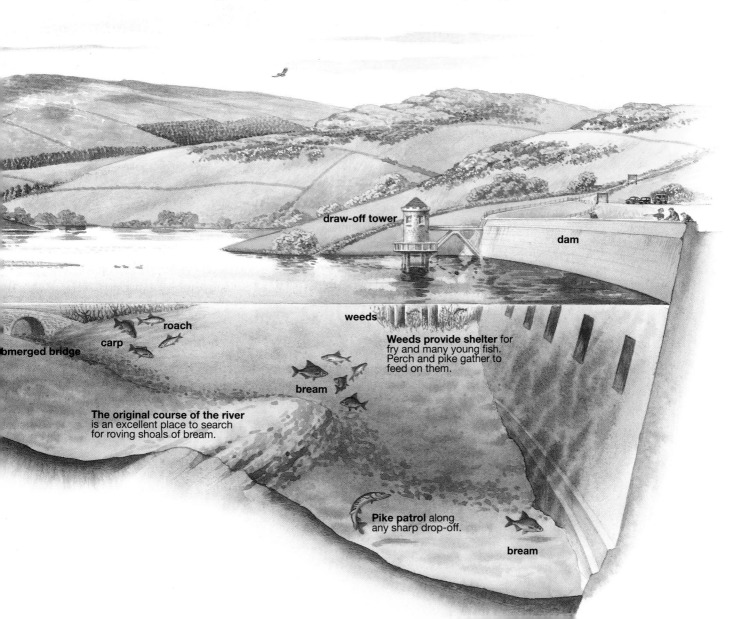

draw-off tower

dam

weeds

Weeds provide shelter for fry and many young fish. Perch and pike gather to feed on them.

roach

carp

submerged bridge

bream

The original course of the river is an excellent place to search for roving shoals of bream.

Pike patrol along any sharp drop-off.

bream

▶ *Rudd are abundant in many reservoirs, where they can grow very large – both of this brace weighed over 1½lb (0.7kg). The two largest British rudd, weighing 4lb 10oz (2.1kg) and 4lb 5oz (1.96kg), were both reservoir fish.*

⚠ Slippery slope

While fishing dam walls or sloping concrete banks, take great care as they can be very slippery, especially during wet weather. Wear shoes with soles that give good grip or you might end up with a wetting, or worse.

▼ *The reservoir inflow is often a hot spot when other areas are unproductive. The water coming in is usually colder and more oxygenated than the main body of water, so try fishing it on hot summer days when oxygen levels are low elsewhere.*

and pike often tend to choose deeper water in summer, while rudd, carp and tench seem to like the shallower areas), the weather often affects fish behaviour.

The main factor to watch for is the wind. In the absence of other signs, make sure you are fishing into the breeze since most species of fish follow the prevailing wind. Don't make the mistake of fishing in the most sheltered and comfortable section of a water when the fish are elsewhere.

When it is hot and water levels are low, most fish become lethargic during the day. This is when night fishing (where permitted) can score heavily. As the temperature falls in the evening, the fish become more active and

may feed right through the night – often in the shallow margins – until the temperature starts to rise again in the morning.

Reservoir fishing

There are no hard and fast rules when it comes to making the most of any feeding fish you find in a reservoir. Choose tackle and tactics according to situation and the fish you're after. Reel line of around 3lb (1.4kg) b.s. is fine for most species in open water, but step this up to 4lb (1.8kg) b.s. around snags. If the fish are being coy, though, you'll need a fine hooklength. The most successful methods are floatfishing and using the swimfeeder.

If you fancy a go at summer pike, the most exciting and productive methods are often sink-and-draw deadbaiting and lure fishing. They help you to cover a lot more ground than static deadbaiting and so are more likely to put you in touch with fish which may only be feeding erratically.

Faced with so much open water, many anglers are tempted to cast as far as they can. The fish however, often feed very close in, among the weeds and silt and can be missed by anglers fishing at great distance. This is especially true at night, when disturbances at the bankside, which tend to drive fish into the shelter of deeper water, are at a minimum. If you follow these few simple rules of thumb, a visit to an unknown reservoir need not be an excuse to blank.

Gravel pits in winter

**John Bailey makes no bones about it:
gravel pit fishing in the depths of winter can be hard and
slow, not least because the fish can be difficult
to find in cold weather. But if you really want specimen
roach, pike or perch, you ignore gravel pits
in winter at your peril, he warns.**

Clear water conditions and relatively low fish populations tend to deter all but the keenest and hardiest anglers from venturing on to the banks of gravel pits in winter.

But enthusiasm and hardiness on their own aren't enough. Only by thinking about your fishing can you cut down on blanks and make the most of your time at the water.

Sometimes you can catch bream, carp and tench – and even very occasionally rudd and eels – but to all intents and purposes gravel pit fishing in winter means roach, pike and perch. The other species just don't feed anything like often enough to make pursuit of them worthwhile to any but the most dedicated single-species fanatic.

Worst weather

Your first and foremost consideration must always be the weather: it's absolutely critical on all still waters in winter.

The worst conditions occur when an area of high pressure settles over the country, bringing clear skies, frosty nights and bright, cold days. Usually there's little or no wind, and when there is it tends to be an icy northerly or easterly.

There are no hard and fast rules, of

▼ *Gravel pits have been called 'barren inland seas' and you can see why on a day like this. A strong wind is no bad thing – just so long as it's from the south or west and not from the north or east.*

Mild, windy days offer the best chance of sport.

Be prepared – warm, waterproof clothes and footwear, a brolly, hot drinks and plenty of food are all essential.

dead reed stalks

roach

perch

WINTER ON A GRAVEL PIT

course, and pike especially sometimes feed on the coldest of days, even during a long freeze when you have to smash holes in the ice...but don't count on it!

Best conditions
The period after a cold snap can be very productive, particularly two or three days after any ice has thawed and the water has warmed up, even if only very slightly.

Ideal conditions, however, occur when an area of low pressure passes over the coun-

try. Constant cloud cover keeps light values down by day and temperatures up at night, while lively winds bring warm air from the south or west. It's on such days that you really must try to be on the bank.

Feeding times
Gravel pit roach, pike and perch tend to feed in spells in winter, even during the most favourable weather. If you don't know when these feeding times are you might sit by the side of a water for hour after biteless

Perch are active on mild days, on the hunt for prey fish like small roach.

> ⚠️ **Be prepared**
>
> Fish when you are cold, wet and hungry and your concentration, enjoyment and health all suffer. Essential defences against the elements are waterproof outer clothing, thermal underwear, thermal boots, a decent brolly, lots of food and flasks of hot drink.
>
> Norwich tackle dealer Dave Plummer reclines on a bedchair under a huge brolly and cooks himself breakfast, lunch and tea on a portable gas stove. Strange how he attracts everyone on the pit...

◀ *Pike grow big in gravel pits. They tend to have fairly fixed feeding times in winter but there are no hard and fast rules. They can come on the feed quite suddenly, then stop feeding again just as unexpectedly.*

island

promontory

pike

pike

plateau

roach

In mild weather roach roam around looking for food carried by strong undertows and are often found over shallow plateaux.

perch

Packs of pike often settle in one place – find it and you could be in for a bumper day's sport.

In very cold spells roach and perch may shoal up tightly in deep, warm holes.

hour only to pack up just as the fish are about to come on the feed.

Roach can feed on and off at any time when the weather's mild but generally they feed best from when the light starts fading late in the afternoon until early evening.

Pike tend to feed at very fixed times. These vary from pit to pit but are generally at first and last light. However, many pits also see a late morning to lunchtime feeding session. A change in weather or light conditions can also trigger an unscheduled feeding spell. For example, a bank of cloud passing across the sun often prompts a pike or two to feed.

Perch can come on the feed at absolutely any time during the day from before it gets light until after darkness falls.

Where to find roach

In mild, windy weather, roach tend to be found wherever there is a strong sub-surface drift; depth is of secondary importance. They wander far and wide looking for food carried by these underwater currents, which are commonly found over relatively shallow plateaux or bars or in gently

▶ *Author John Bailey – wrapped up securely against the cold – with a big, brazen perch taken from a gravel pit on a winter's day.*

▲ *The worst conditions for any still water, not just gravel pits – though there are days when you can catch through holes in the ice.*

Main methods

Feeder-fishing can hardly be bettered for roach. To find a likely swim on a mild day, rove along the bank, casting out a large empty feeder until you feel it being swept around by a strong undertow.

When the water is clear, as it usually is in gravel pits in winter, pike feed mainly by sight and livebaiting is impossible to beat. Deadbaiting is usually only the best method when wind and rain colours the water and the pike feed more by scent than sight.

Drifting the bait under a large, vaned float is an effective way of covering a lot of water, increasing your chances of intercepting a roaming pike and – if you are lucky – finding a hotspot where a pack of pike has gathered. Generally, baits suspended in mid-water work better than those fished on the bottom.

A small, free-roaming, floatfished livebait is a good method for big perch but a legered deadbait is more likely to catch the fish of a lifetime. Always use a wire trace in case a pike takes the bait.

▼ *Dawn is usually one of the best times to catch gravel pit pike in winter but you have to be dedicated to haul yourself out of bed.*

contoured bays around the margins.

When the weather is cold and still, roach are much less active and tend to shoal up in the comparatively warm water of deep holes, which can be anywhere from the middle of the pit to right under the bank.

Tracking down pike

Pike, too, are most active in mild weather, when they roam the pit, following the gullies in a slow, steady search for food.

Frequently a pack of pike gathers and settles in a particular area and a hotspot is formed. This may be where there is a concentration of small prey fish, or where there are features such as snags.

Often, though, there is no obvious explanation for a hotspot and the more water you can cover the greater your chance of finding one.

Pinpointing perch

Traditional wisdom is that perch sit out the winter in the deepest parts of the pit. This may be the case in very cold weather but in milder spells the striped shoals roam all over the pit searching for food. It's common to see a perch chasing a small, skipping single fish along the surface, its distinctive dorsal fin proud of the water.

Fishing lakes by boat

Potteries angler Graham Marsden is an expert on the Shropshire and Cheshire meres. Here he tells you how to track down fish on large open waters.

Tip Ship-shape

On a boat always keep essential items of tackle laid out within easy reach before you start fishing. You don't want to be stumbling about and rocking the boat when the fish are in the swim.

▼ *Fishing from the bank has its good points but when it comes to freedom and mobility there's nothing to beat a punt. You can fish all the parts you can't reach from the bank.*

Fishing the open waters of lakes and meres can be a daunting prospect. Typically you are met with an expanse of water which – apart from marginal vegetation – has no features that might give you a clue where the fish are.

Often, though, it is in the open water where many species spend their lives – especially on waters where the banks are busy with people strolling about. Even where bankside activity is minimal, some species (particularly bream) prefer to feed well out from the margins.

Modern tackle and techniques have made it easier to cast great distances, but long-distance fishing still has its problems. It is far easier to go looking for the fish in a boat, and you can then use the most delicate of techniques that long-distance bank fishing prohibits. Make sure that you have the permission of any riparian landowners and the necessary licences before launching your punt.

Messing about in boats

Flat-bottomed punts are the best boats from which to fish. They are stable, safe, and enable you to fish from a comfortable chair. Their only disadvantage is that they are not the easiest of crafts to manoeuvre – especially when it's windy.

If you have no access to a punt, then the next best thing is a river boat – either clinker-built or glass-fibre. River boats are not as stable or comfortable as punts but they are much easier to handle.

Run silent Whatever type of boat you use, line the bottom with carpet. This serves two purposes: it deadens noise so that you are less likely to scare the fish, and it is kinder on the fish when you lay them down to unhook them.

Tie up, anchor down Anchoring the boat at both ends stops it from swinging around. Mud anchors are best. They need be no more than blocks of concrete inset with eye bolts. They should weigh between 20-30lb (9-14kg) and be attached with nylon ropes. Make sure the ropes are at least 1.8m (6ft) longer than the deepest water in the lake.

◀ *Lake margins are sometimes more attractive to the angler than the fish. Don't neglect the large expanses of featureless open water – they often hold some very large specimens.*

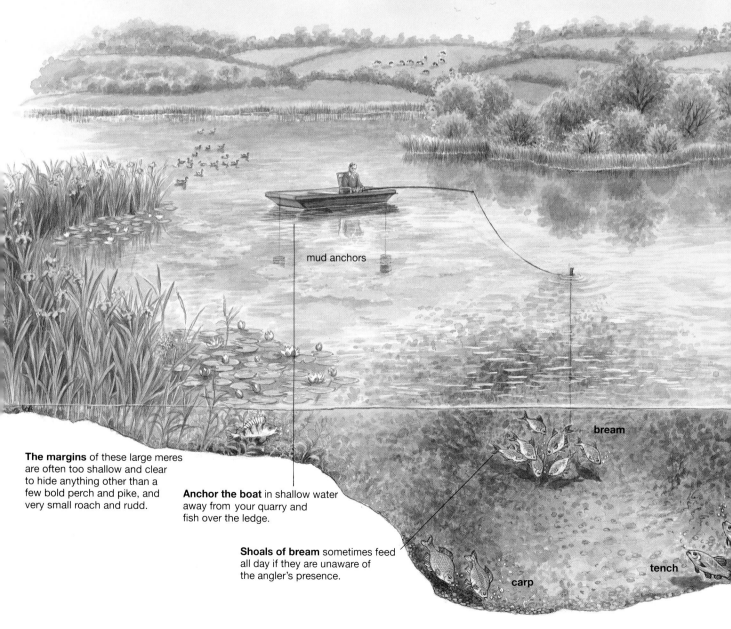

mud anchors

The margins of these large meres are often too shallow and clear to hide anything other than a few bold perch and pike, and very small roach and rudd.

Anchor the boat in shallow water away from your quarry and fish over the ledge.

Shoals of bream sometimes feed all day if they are unaware of the angler's presence.

bream

carp

tench

For safety's sake always treat boats with respect. Never stand up in them unnecessarily; never clown around and always wear a life jacket. Even the shallowest waters can be dangerous. Don't go out when it's rough.

Fish location

Before you can find the fish you need to know a little about their environment.

Making a depth chart is a great help. The easiest way is to use a sonar device. The simple clock face, depth only, read-out type is quite good enough for this. Failing this, a float and plummet are just as accurate but take much longer.

In order to make a rough chart you need to pick out landmarks around the lake. These can be trees, electricity pylons, distant hills – anything in fact.

Line up the boat so that it lies between two opposing landmarks – this positions the boat along a line. To fix your position, line up with two more opposing landmarks (at 90° to the first two). Take a depth read-

▲ *Graham Marsden carefully slips back a big bream into a Cheshire mere. Many lakes hold fish like this but it takes planning and patience to get them on the bank (or boat).*

ing and make a note of this on a plan of the lake. (The plan needs to have the landmarks drawn in.) By systematically repeating this process you can 'break' the lake into a series of grids.

What to do with the chart It is the precise character of a lake bottom that is of interest to the angler and, in particular, any feature that deviates from the plain bed of the lake.

The most common features are deep, basin-like depressions and ledges where the bottom suddenly dips away into deeper water. These are important because they are the natural feeding areas and patrol routes for many species. Bream, tench, roach and carp all love these spots. These fish in turn attract pike and perch which are able to use the features to ambush their prey.

The angler's quarry Before choosing baits and techniques you need to decide which species to go for. It is no use fishing for tench if there are only a few in the lake. So how do you decide? One way is to find out from the local anglers, bailiffs, tackle shops and newspapers what the dominant species are. Another way is to observe the water as often as possible during the first two hours of daylight and note which species roll at the surface. (This also tells you exactly where the fish are.) If all else fails, try fishing 'blind' with a bait like maggots that is attractive to all types of fish (except pike) and just see what turns up.

Reputation You usually find that waters gain reputations for producing certain

In truly open, featureless water, where there are no signs of fish rolling, it is often necessary to pre-bait days in advance.

Shallow water around rush islands is excellent for rudd and pike.

Deep basin-like depressions are home to shoals of bream, tench and carp.

OPEN WATER ON A MEDIUM DEPTH LAKE

Cheshire and Shropshire meres

Many lakes and meres are not controlled by clubs and can be fished by boat if permission for launching a boat is sought from riparian landowners first. Make sure you have the appropriate water authority licence.

● **Ellesmere, Shropshire** Day ticket punt fishing is available on at least one of the meres. Information available from the warden Sian Costello (0691 623 461).

● **Petty Pool, Cheshire** Controlled by Mid Cheshire Angler's Association. Day tickets available from local tackle shops. Boat fishing available by permission from the club secretary.

● **Pickmere, Cheshire** Controlled by Northwich A.A. Enquire Scott's Tackle, Northwich.

▶ *It is an early June morning. You are anchored near the prebaited swim and have just caught the first fish – a tench like the one on the right. This is what fishing is all about!*

species – becoming known as carp, bream or tench waters, for example. So it makes sense to choose a species according to the water's reputation and then concentrate on the features mentioned above.

Fishing the ledge A swim with a distinct ledge is an excellent one to try from a boat. By anchoring back from the ledge in shallow water but within a comfortable float cast, you are out of sight of the fish but still close enough to be able to loose feed. When you hook a fish, pull it up and over the ledge as quickly as possible so that the commotion doesn't disturb the rest of the shoal.

Featureless waters Where there is no distinct ledge it is best to fish as far away from the swim as possible. Just how far away you fish depends on how far you can fire loose feed with your catapult.

On featureless waters where you have not seen any signs of fish movement – surface rolling or mud clouding – it would be wise to prebait the chosen spot for several days before fishing with samples of the hookbait.

Lake tactics

Precisely which tackle you choose depends on the species you are after, but for roach, rudd, bream, tench, carp and perch,

floatfishing combined with loose feeding is about the deadliest combination.

For calm conditions use insert wagglers; in windy conditions drift-beaters are best. Use line from 2-6lb (0.9-2.7kg) b.s according to the size and species you are hoping to catch. Choose your hook size to suit the bait. (These are usually maggots, casters, corn, bread, or fish for pike.)

▼ *There are literally thousands of lakes like this one – just waiting to be fished. But to get the best out of a venue it pays to concentrate on one water and spend time getting to know it really well.*

Freshwater docks

Docks like those of London and Bristol offer excellent fishing. Top London angler Les Hammond reveals a range of methods for tackling the teeming docklands.

Deep waters

Take extra care when fishing docks as their depth makes them very dangerous. If you're anything less than a good swimmer, wear a life-jacket or fish with someone who can swim well. Do not play silly or dangerous games around docks – accidents do happen and they can have tragic consequences.
If you're a junior always go with an adult.

Freshwater docks have always tended to hold huge heads of fish. Even in the days when they were busy with ships being unloaded and there was a constant film of surface oil and other debris, fish thrived.

Yet, at first glance, coarse fishing in freshwater docks can appear a daunting task to the newcomer. Many anglers never even consider wetting a line in such virtually featureless, often vast, expanses of water.

Fishing in freshwater docks is an art in itself. The angler not only has to learn where the fish are, but also discover how the fish feed. There are almost no giveaway signs. You won't find overhanging trees, lily patches, weed beds or any of the normal clues to good fish areas.

At best there may be some disused machinery or moored boats offering fish shelter, but even these are unlikely. Dumped cranes are vanishing as the docks are cleaned up and the boats are only temporary placements – their very presence being a sign of the varied uses our docks are now being put to. Undeveloped docks often feature sunken boats and machinery on the bottom. These give useful cover to fish – but can cause snags.

Many a docker once used his place of work for a little angling recreation. Today the docks are largely silent, or subject to all manner of development. Nevertheless the fish are still there.

Think deep

Because they were built to house large boats there is no such thing as shallow water in a dock. With the majority the bottom is at least 3.7m (12ft) down and they are sometimes as deep as 12m (40ft).

You could describe docks, from a fishing angle, as featureless concrete holes in the ground – with sheer sides going down to a

▼ *Always ask at local tackle shops if you need permission to fish. Many docks are available only on a club ticket.*

Abandoned boats offer fish welcome shelter.

Freshwater docks are home to vast shoals of bream and roach.

Pike lurk in ambush behind any obstacles they can find.

Dumped machinery and other items give cover for fish.

There are rich pickings to be had on the bottom for such fish as bream.

Tip *Dock tackle*

For float fishing Les uses a 13ft (4m) soft-actioned match rod – with 3lb (1.4kg) line, 3AAA to 3SSG slider floats, size 16-20 hooks and 1½-2lb (0.7-0.9kg) hooklengths.

fairly flat bottom. Different docks vary little in appearance – the only change being in size, which can range from an acre or two to truly enormous areas of water.

All manner of fish inhabit freshwater docks. There are often vast shoals of bream, roach, tench, rudd, pike, and perch, while some docks are also the home of huge carp. Even typical running water species such as chub and dace can be commonplace. Some of the London docks have big heads of dace, which have no doubt worked their way in from the Thames and other connecting waterways.

Despite the bleakness of their surroundings, the fish are usually in mint condition, with a plumpness that reveals a good diet.

Going to the wall

One prime natural source of food for these

Fish can be caught
summer and winter –
but vary their
feeding depth.

Freshwater shrimp –
a key food source
– are found around
dock walls.

Walls provide
algae, a good
natural food for
roach.

FINDING THE FISH IN DOCKLAND

shade or cover, however slight, are also well
worth trying.

In summer dock fish gather in the
warmest layer of water, usually between
the surface and half way down. On very hot
days you may even see fish cruising along
the surface. As temperatures fall through
autumn and into winter, the fish change
their habitat and drop deeper into the
water, being found right at the bottom in
the coldest weather. They don't go away,

*▲ Typical London
regenerated docklands – the
point where a river joins the
docks area is often a good
place to find feeding fish.*

*▼ In areas such as Surrey
Docks you may well be
successful fishing near the
wall – it's home to many
food sources.*

fish is the algae that is always found in
abundance on and around the dock walls.
Because of this you probably won't have to
fish too far from the dock edge. Freshwater
shrimps also frequent the area near the
walls – they are another good source of food
for dock fish.

If you are a newcomer, fishing docks for
the first time, start off by getting to work
with a plummet to establish the sort of
depth you are going to fish. Good starting
points are any inlets there may be – either
from connecting canals or the main river.
These are often excellent holding points for
fish. Areas where there is some form of

▲ *When fishing docklands the angler will have to get used to large featureless expanses of water. It seems an obvious point but check that the area you're fishing is unpolluted freshwater.*

▼ *Typical fish in London's docks are tench, roach, bream – and rudd, like this fine example. Docks hold large shoals of such fish – so a day's angling can be very productive.*

though – the beauty of dock fishing is that most venues respond summer and winter.

Choose your style

Docks lend themselves well to three styles of fishing – the long pole with fixed line, sliding float on rod and reel, and the feeder with a quivertip rod.

The long pole is the best way of fishing at a fixed depth. In the summer, when the fish are likely to be feeding up in the water a lightly shotted float – giving the bait a slow drop through to the depth being fished – can be excellent. When the fish are feeding deep

an Olivette rig with a couple of droppers below is the best method.

The sliding float For searching out fish in summer or winter, the sliding float is hard to beat – it enables the bait to be dropped right through the water. When using the slider, always have a biggish shot – between a no.1 and a BB – as a tell-tale dropper to give a solid indication should you take any fish on the drop.

Be sure to use a proper sliding knot when fishing this method – leave the ends cut long so as not to impede the passage of line through the rod rings. The knot can be easily adjusted to give a fixed depth if the fish are all taking at one level.

The swimfeeder When fishing a swimfeeder use an open-end type packed with groundbait and a few samples of the hookbait. With this method always cast to the same spot each time. This builds up a carpet of feed to hold foraging fish. 'Twitching' the bait along the bottom with quarter turns of the reel handle often encourages a bite.

Large maggots are the best all-round bait – with casters, bread, and worms next on the list of preference. Bread and worms work well with the feeder, and can often sort out some good quality fish – but it is the more commonly used maggots and casters that can take the most.

When fishing maggots and casters, always keep a steady stream of loose-feed samples going in. You don't have to use a lot – six to a dozen a time is enough – but they must be fed every few minutes to keep the fish interested.

Autumn still waters – finding the mobile fish

Autumn: perhaps the best time to be out with your rods – the days are mild and fish feed freely... but some days they are frustratingly elusive. Find out why with Nigel Witham.

◀ *Big carp like this, and a host of other species, feed freely in autumn, once the sweltering days of summer are just a memory. But remember, they tend to roam widely in most still waters at this time of year.*

▼ *Autumn often provides the very best of prolific pike sport as the fish feed up before winter. Put at least one of your baits alongside an old reed or weed bed – both prey fish and predator hide there.*

It's autumn – the summer crowds are gone, the countryside is at its most beautiful and the fish are feeding hard in preparation for winter. But you've got to find them first.

Better to spend three hours looking for the fish and an hour fishing the right place than to fish a barren spot for four hours. It sounds like hard work, and it is, so how about some simple science to make it easier?

Fish preferences

As summer fades, fish adapt their behaviour to the changing conditions. The water cools as the nights grow longer. Cold water can hold more dissolved oxygen than warm water, so oxygen levels in autumn are always within the fish's preferred limits. The simmering days of summer when the fish bask and won't bite are gone.

Like us, fish aren't too keen on the cold, so once the oxygen level is adequate they seek the warmest water. Find that, and you've generally found the fish too. In autumn, water temperatures tend to vary widely and the fish adapt their behaviour to suit. To help you follow the fishes' movements, a thermometer you can cast into the water is a vital piece of equipment.

Weird water

Water is a peculiar liquid in at least two ways. Firstly, it takes a long time to change temperature – much longer than air. So in early autumn the water is almost at summer temperatures, even after a day or two of really cold weather. Later on, however,

On warm sunny days rudd, carp, tench and chub (if there are any) move into the shallow water – unless you disturb them.

tench

carp

Most fish species hide and feed in among the remains of the summer's weed beds – especially potamogeton and lilies with heavy root systems.

Carp and tench enjoy a good root around in the mud, searching for small food items such as insect larvae and snails.

AN AUTUMNAL LAKE

Tip Light effects

When fishing an unfamiliar water, travel light and aim to fish half a dozen swims for an hour or two each. It's the best way to explore the water, finding holes, weed beds and snags. Obviously, stick to a swim if you're catching.

▼ *Windy days are the norm in autumn and wind can have a profound effect on fishing – not just because it causes drag. Wind can push the warm water around – and the fish tend to follow it.*

when the water has cooled to more like winter temperatures, even a couple of days of mild weather doesn't warm the water up more than a fraction.

Water's second strange habit is its behaviour as it cools. Above 4°C (39°F) it's just like any other liquid – the colder it gets, the denser it becomes – cold water sinks. So in early to mid-autumn, before water has cooled to below this temperature, the warmest water is in the top layer.

Later on, when the water has cooled to this temperature, strange things happen. Below 4°C (39°F) water actually gets less dense as it cools – the opposite to what it did before. So in autumn, as the water at the surface cools to below this temperature, it floats on the denser water underneath (which is at 4°C/39°F), instead of sinking.

The warmest water is therefore at the bottom. In many waters, the temperature there stays at 4°C (39°F) from autumn right through to spring, unless the weather is very harsh or the still water very shallow.

That's why fish tend to gather in the deepest areas. Perch in particular, form tight shoals and gradually migrate to the deepest spots, because they're the warmest.

However, the surface layers (and shallow water) do change temperature a little faster. So on mild, sunny days these areas warm up most quickly, no matter how cold the rest of the water.

If the temperature in these places climbs above 4°C (39°F), or it's still early autumn, look for fish, especially rudd, chub, carp and tench, in the warmer, shallower water. You can catch them there if you don't disturb them first. But on chilly days, these areas are cold and fishless.

Tip Brave the winds for eels

"Are you keen to catch a specimen eel?" asks Nigel Witham. "Try fishing the first blustery weather of autumn, which usually occurs at the end of September or the beginning of October. This is possibly the very best time to catch a really big eel.

"At this time they are often caught in numbers from waters where they are hardly ever taken in high summer. Some anglers think this is because it's the time of year when eels get ready to migrate back to the sea. I don't know whether that's right or not, but I've certainly caught more specimens at the beginning of autumn and in these sorts of conditions than at any other time. Try legering a big juicy lobworm in a deep hole on the lake bed."

eel

pike

Fish feed in many
different spots around
a still water in autumn,
depending on conditions.

When the water cools in late
autumn, most fish congregate
in the deepest areas where
the water is warmest.

perch

Pike hang around snags and
concentrations of small fish.

▲ *An angler steers a quality stillwater roach
towards his waiting net. Autumn sport is
often superb once you locate the shoals.*

Using the wind

Autumn is a period often associated with
windy weather. Strong winds can stir up
the water so that it is all the same temperature. If they are less severe they tend to
blow any warm water at the surface to the
downwind bank – and the fish follow.

If the water is less than 4°C (39°F) at the
surface, the warmer water at the bottom
may be pushed back towards the upwind
bank by the colder surface water collecting
at the downwind bank. This is quite rare,
but when it does happen the fishing is often
best with the wind at your back.

That's a gas

Come October, the trees begin to lose their
leaves. Some anglers prefer to avoid tree-
lined areas, believing that fish don't like
decomposing leaf litter or that they won't
find the bait for leaves.

However, the bubbles you see all season
are methane gas – a by-product of decomposing leaves and other detritus. This process continues all year but it's slower during
cold weather because the bacteria that
cause it are less active. So if anything, avoid
these areas in summer, not autumn.

Which waters

All of the above applies to every type of still
water but there are some more specific
points to bear in mind.

Tip Weather works

Approach the bank with
caution on warm days. If
you're quiet you'll catch
fish in the margins. Setting
up in comfort might be a
bit harder, but it'll put
more fish on the bank.

When it's cold, many
anglers use small baits,
such as maggot, in the
belief that fishes' digestive
systems work more slowly,
leading them to prefer
small meals.

Nigel has found the
exact opposite to be true.
Because fish are sluggish,
they prefer a big meal
which lasts them a long
time so they don't have to
keep foraging for food. In a
cold spell, stick to big
baits, such as a juicy
wriggling lobworm.

If you have a choice of
venue on a windy day, pick
a tree-lined one. Wind can
make fishing difficult on
exposed waters, causing
drag, a nasty chop, and
making casting harder.

◀ *This angler obviously knows the contours of the lake bed. Information of this kind can make the difference between exciting autumn action and depressing inactivity.*

With lakes and reservoirs formed by damming a stream, it's usually quite easy to work out the contours. The deep water is always by the dam and the deepest of all is where the old stream bed lies. If you can find this you will almost certainly find a regular hotspot for the coldest days.

On the oldest lakes the stream bed may have been filled in by deposition, but there is nearly always something left. It's a great help if you are lucky enough to have a boat with an echo sounder (and permission to use it). If not, then it's back to hard work with the plummet.

On gravel pits and other workings, such as clay and chalk pits, the underwater profile can be quite different from the one you'd expect to find in estate lakes, ponds and reservoirs which are generally deep in the middle and shallow near the edges.

Gravel pits often have shallow areas away from the banks and any deep water between these shallows is often a hotspot. If the pit you fish is large, wait until the close season when there is time to plumb accurately without disturbing others.

◀ *Don't neglect feeding once you've engaged your brain and worked out where the fish are. You've still got to make them feed and keep them interested in your hookbait.*

▼ *The result of all that hard work selecting the right swim to fish in autumn is often a decent catch or a good specimen such as this lovely perch – proudly displayed by Bruno Broughton.*

Undercover fish

Having found the general area in which to fish, don't forget the usual pointers. Tench and carp prefer a muddy bottom but most other species like a hard clay or gravel bed.

Look for cover – especially old tree stumps in the water and reed and lily beds, which die back in the autumn. *Potamogeton* is a lily-like weed with very small dark green leaves on the surface. Most species of fish love to hide in it.

Whatever species of fish you want to catch, it pays to add the ability to use water temperatures to your armoury of water craft skills. If you do, autumn will become your favourite time of year.

Reservoirs in winter

The reservoirs of England and Wales, whether of the concrete-sided or drowned-valley type, can provide a rich source of winter sport – as Jon Culley sets out to prove.

The reservoirs made by damming a small brook or stream which then floods the surrounding valley are a joy to anglers because they are so scenic. The other type of reservoir is completely man-made and has sloping concrete banks. While these are nowhere near as attractive to look at as the 'natural' flooded-valley type, the fishing in them can be just as good.

Finding the features

At first you may think that there is no real way of locating the fish in a big reservoir in winter. Though it seems that all you can do is 'chuck-it-and-chance-it', this is far from the case.

The fish-finding features on a reservoir are not as obvious as on some other waters. There are no islands or bars just visible below the surface and most weedbeds have died off come winter (if, in fact, there were any there in the summer).

The only visible features are the dam wall and valve tower – both of which can provide excellent sport in winter.

From the dam wall you can reach the deep water easily. A lot of fish gather here in winter, attracted by food particles trapped in the deep water at the bottom of the wall.

The valve tower provides fish with both

protection and food. Coarse fish find plenty to eat among the algae growing around the base and up the sides of the tower – and the algae shelter lots of insects, on which roach and bream feed. The protection of the valve tower also attracts a host of small fish and fry in winter and these, in turn, draw the two prime predators – pike and perch.

Below the surface on drowned-valley reservoirs, features such as hedgerows, roads and fences, old farm buildings or submerged bridges over the old stream bed can

▲ Cold and bleak it may be – but there's no reason why you shouldn't bag up on waters like this in winter.

On the drowned-valley type of reservoir, below-the-surface features such as hedgerows or old buildings are good fish holding areas.

Check these out on old maps or ask local anglers where the hotspots are.

▼ A sudden mild spell in winter is often the very best time to fish – the rise in temperature can bring most fish on to the feed.

Really mild conditions can even tempt shoals of roach back into the shallows for a while, though they normally prefer the deeper stretches of water in the winter.

◄ There's no need to despair if you find ice on the water when you arrive – allow a couple of hours for the sun to melt it, and you could be on for a bumper catch.

Old buildings provide good fish holding areas.

Pike prefer the deeper water in winter.

Winter hotspots

● **Ardingly Res., Sussex**
Trout water open to coarse anglers in winter. Pike to over 30lb (13.6kg). Many roach, some perch. Apply: C. Simpson, The Lodge, Ardingly Reservoir, West Sussex (Tel. 0444 892549).

● **Ardleigh Res., Essex**
Trout water open in winter for coarse fishing – pike over 44lb (20kg), perch to 3lb (1.3kg), many roach. Apply Fisheries Officer, Ardleigh Reservoir, Colchester, Essex.

● **Damflask Res., Sheffield** Trout water, also open for coarse fishing – pike to 34lb (15.4kg); most coarse fish. Day tickets from machines on bank.

● **Knipton Res., Melton Mowbray, Leics** Good pike, roach and bream. Day tickets: Club HQ at Rutland Arms, King Street.

● **Staunton Harold Res., Derbys** Double figure pike, roach and perch to 2lb (0.9kg), bream to 6lb (2.7kg). Day tickets: Melbourne Tackle and Gun, High Street, Melbourne.

● **Sywell Res., Northants** Pike over 20lb (9kg); roach and perch. Tickets: local tackle shops.

● **Tring Reservoirs, Herts** Three reservoirs: pike of 30lb (13.6kg), roach to nearly 4lb (1.8kg). Tickets: B. Double, Watery Lane, Marsworth, Herts, or telephone Tring 2379.

▲ Fishing Wintersett Reservoir, Yorkshire in winter. For safety's sake, wrap up warm, carry spare dry clothing and go equipped with food and a flask of hot soup, coffee or tea.

provide excellent fish holding areas. They are best located by looking at old maps of the area before it was flooded – or by talking to local anglers. (Concrete bowl reservoirs lack most of these features.)

If you get permission to take a boat out on to the reservoir, then an echo-sounder can be an invaluable piece of equipment. Look for contours on the bottom, such as troughs and ledges, or for the course of the old stream bed. All can hold fish.

Sudden drops-offs are among the best areas to locate shoals of coarse fish. A carefully positioned bait at the bottom of a drop-off can be most productive.

Watch the weather

During the colder winter months beware of fishing the shallows. When the weather is really cold the shallows on the reservoir are almost completely devoid of fish, so there is little point in wasting time fishing these areas. To quote an old saying "You can't catch the fish if they are not there" – although if there is a sudden mild spell the fish may move back into some of the

LOCATING RESERVOIR FISH IN WINTER

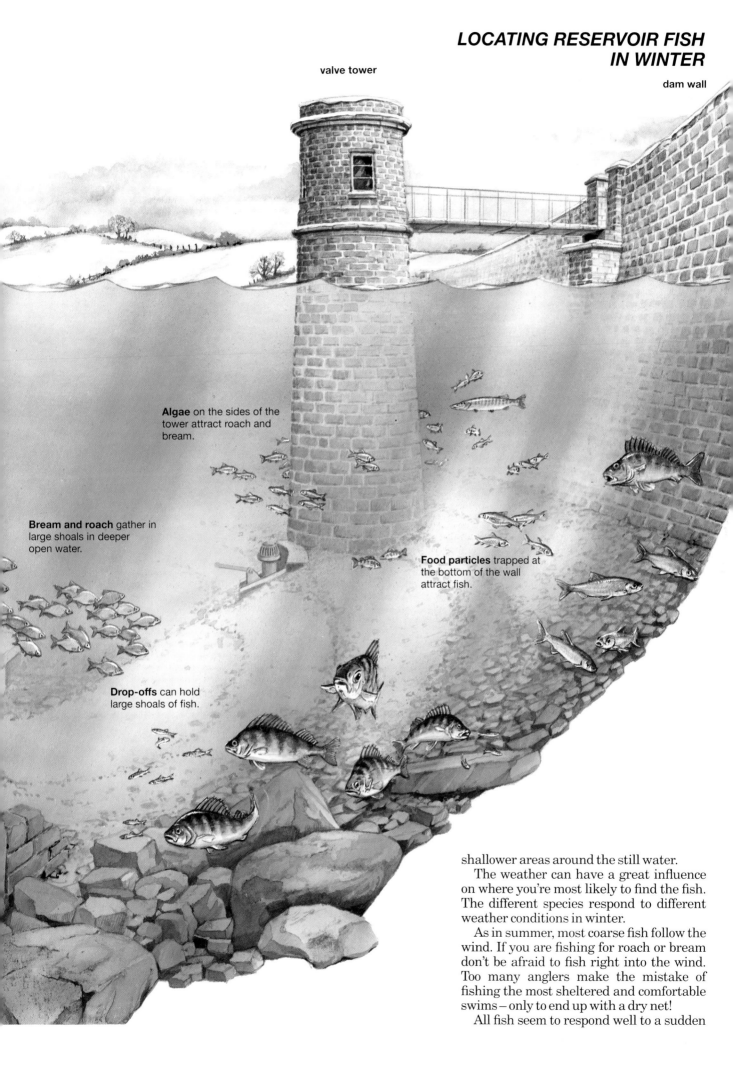

valve tower

dam wall

Algae on the sides of the tower attract roach and bream.

Bream and roach gather in large shoals in deeper open water.

Food particles trapped at the bottom of the wall attract fish.

Drop-offs can hold large shoals of fish.

shallower areas around the still water.

The weather can have a great influence on where you're most likely to find the fish. The different species respond to different weather conditions in winter.

As in summer, most coarse fish follow the wind. If you are fishing for roach or bream don't be afraid to fish right into the wind. Too many anglers make the mistake of fishing the most sheltered and comfortable swims – only to end up with a dry net!

All fish seem to respond well to a sudden

◄ *Wilstone Reservoir, Tring, Hertfordshire – an excellent winter venue for big pike, roach and bream. Any areas that provide some shelter are good places to search for the fish.*

Try for roach and bream at dawn or in the evening, using lobworms, bread or maggots.

▼ *Big shoals of roach haunt the dam walls and valve towers in reservoirs, attracted there by rich supplies of algae and insects. They also swim in the deeper open water.*

Rough, windy weather, when the water is coloured, provides ideal conditions for catching them.

▲ *The species to go for in winter on a reservoir has got to be the pike – it is possible to catch specimens like this 21½lb (9.7kg) beauty in most weather and with either livebaits or deadbaits.*

rise in temperature. If it has been cold for a length of time, then a sudden mild spell, when the higher temperature brings most fish on to the feed, is the best time to fish.

A sudden cold snap has just the opposite effect – putting most of the fish off the feed until the temperature has stabilized after a few days.

The fish to look for

The main species in reservoirs are pike, perch, roach and bream.

Pike This fish is probably the most obliging feeder of them all. It feeds right through the winter in all types of weather and conditions, from the mild October winds to the frost and snow in the heart of winter – although sport does become slower as the

weather turns colder. In the winter pike prefer the deeper water, with the dam and valve tower being hotspots. And wherever you can find shoals of small fish or fry, the pike will not be far away.

All standard methods can catch pike on reservoirs, with either livebaits or deadbaits being the most successful. A drift float can come in useful for reaching those areas, such as sudden drop-offs, which are out of casting reach.

Perch Like the pike, you can find the perch wherever there are fry, but they also like snaggy areas such as the valve tower or sunken buildings and walls where there is the chance of some shelter.

Best baits for perch are lobworms, small livebaits or deadbaits or spinners. Do not fish for perch during the really cold months. The best times are October until early December, before the hard frosts start to set in, and February and March when the weather turns milder towards the end of the season.

Bream and roach These two species have very similar habits during the winter. Both swim around in big shoals in the deeper open water or by the dam wall. The bream also like to patrol along the course of the old stream bed. Neither species likes the temperature too cold. The best conditions are rough and windy weather when the water has coloured up after heavy rain.

Lobworms, bread and maggots are the best baits for bream and roach. Ideally these baits should be fished at first light and in the evening up to a few hours after dark (if allowed).

CHAPTER TWO

FINDING FISH
IN RIVERS

Fast, clear rivers

Fast, clear rivers, like the famous Hampshire Avon, with their strong flows and dense streamer weed, are a challenge for any angler, but the rewards are there in the shape of big fish.

Dave Plummer

Dave Plummer made his reputation as a big fish angler on the rivers of his native Yorkshire. Ten years ago he moved to Norfolk where he now does much fishing on his favourite river, the Wensum.

▼ *A fast, clear river such as the Hampshire Avon is no place for light tackle – here an angler fishes the Pipes swim on the Royalty.*

Many anglers are put off by the sheer pace of a fast-flowing river. There is also something of a misconception generally that coarse fish don't like fast water. The truth is that fast water might deter anglers but it doesn't bother most coarse fish in the least. After all, they've been around long enough to get used to it! Even in a flood, when the river is belting through, you can see fish rolling on the surface in the fastest mid-stream flow.

The very highest reaches of a river are usually shallow and fairly narrow, and rarely have many features. The water is pure and well oxygenated, and may often harbour brown trout, with perhaps a few dace and minnows.

Moving downstream, the river deepens and widens, and more features begin to appear. The water is fast and clear, and home to barbel, chub, dace, roach, pike and perch, and sometimes even the odd bream.

Which fish where?

Fish are likely to be found anywhere that offers some form of cover and a supply of

food. Under overhanging bushes and trees, in the tails of islands, behind bridge supports, between beds of streamer weed and under sheer banks on the outside of bends are all good for barbel, chub and dace.

Other fish, though not uncomfortable in the main stream, prefer slacker water. Eddies, the insides of bends, and junctions between smaller streams and the main river are good places to look for roach, pike, perch and bream, though pike will hold up in surprisingly fast water so long as it is fairly deep. Bream can provide surprises, too, by showing up in swims more usually associated with barbel, chub and dace.

Surface signs

Once the river has grown to a size where you can no longer see the bottom you have to be able to read the surface signs that indicate where the fish might be.

A flat, smooth surface indicates a flat sand and gravel bed. On summer evenings and nights especially, barbel and chub move on to these flats to feed.

Boulders, logs and other large obstructions on the river bed can be detected by turbulence a few yards downstream. These can be very productive spots for barbel and chub, which both love snags. But they are often the most difficult places to cast to and often result in lost tackle and fish.

Creases – those lines in the surface flow where fast current meets slower – are good places for all fish but especially chub, roach and dace. The fish hang just in the slacker water, conserving energy, only darting in and out of the faster flow for food.

The most difficult spots to find are holes or slight depressions in the river bed that show no surface current variation. These very productive places, especially for barbel and chub, can only be found by plumbing.

Features of a typical fast-flowing river

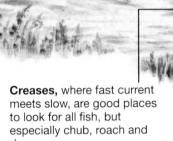

Bridge supports create slightly slower areas of water where barbel, chub and dace can rest out of the main flow, waiting for passing titbits of food.

Islands, like bridge supports, offer barbel, chub and dace slight shelter from the main current and a vantage point from which to wait for passing food.

Creases, where fast current meets slow, are good places to look for all fish, but especially chub, roach and dace.

Eddies, with their slack water, are one of the preferred haunts of roach, pike and perch.

Slack water on the insides of bends is worth trying for roach, perch and pike, which prefer to keep out of the main flow.

Fishing fast-flowing rivers

Time	Fish	Location	Techniques
Summer	Barbel, chub	Fast water	Freelining; trotting; swimfeedering; rolling leger
Autumn	Barbel, chub, dace, pike, perch	Main flow	Trotting; swimfeedering; legering; spinning, livebaiting and deadbaiting for perch and pike
Winter	Chub, roach, dace, pike	Slacker water, holes, creases, eddies	Trotting; swimfeedering; legering; laying on; livebaiting and deadbaiting for pike
Back end	Barbel, chub, roach, dace, pike, perch	Moving back to faster water pre-spawning	All methods

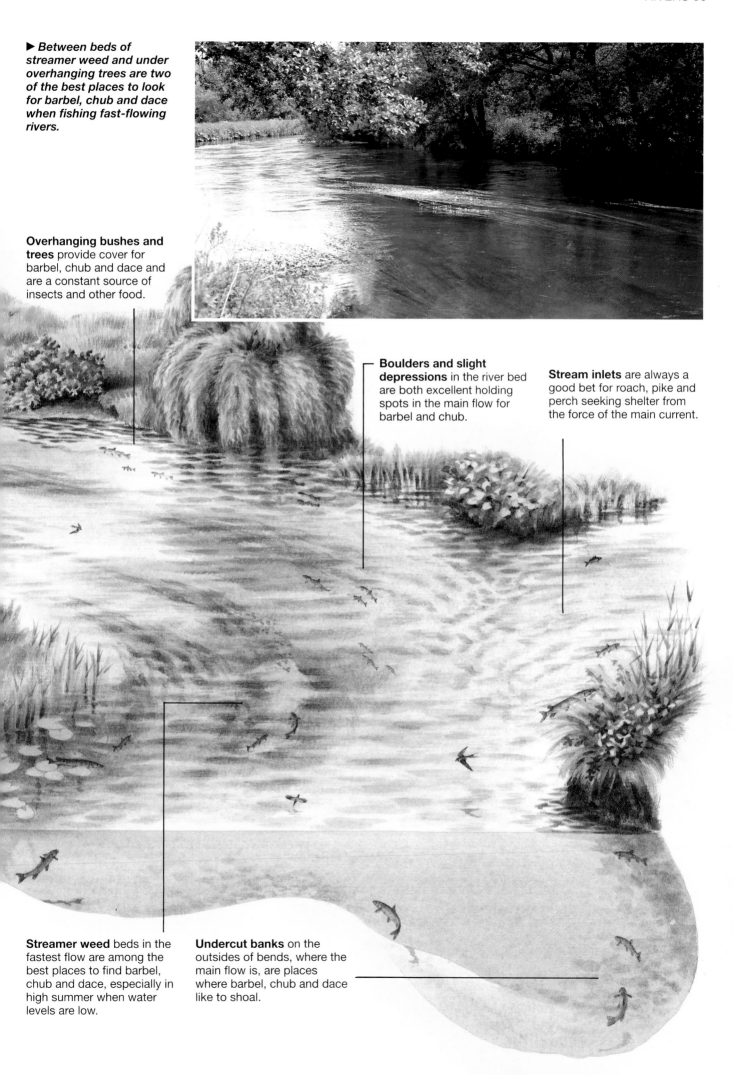

▶ *Between beds of streamer weed and under overhanging trees are two of the best places to look for barbel, chub and dace when fishing fast-flowing rivers.*

Overhanging bushes and trees provide cover for barbel, chub and dace and are a constant source of insects and other food.

Boulders and slight depressions in the river bed are both excellent holding spots in the main flow for barbel and chub.

Stream inlets are always a good bet for roach, pike and perch seeking shelter from the force of the main current.

Streamer weed beds in the fastest flow are among the best places to find barbel, chub and dace, especially in high summer when water levels are low.

Undercut banks on the outsides of bends, where the main flow is, are places where barbel, chub and dace like to shoal.

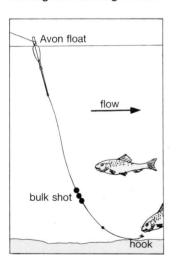

▲ *Barbel like this 8½lb (3.8kg) Hampshire Avon specimen love to hang in the current between beds of streamer weed, waiting for food to pass by.*

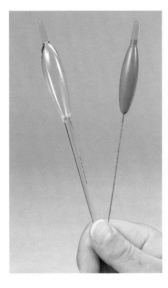

▲ *Avon floats are ideal for trotting fast-flowing water.*

Changing seasons

Fish move to different parts of the river as the year progresses.

Summer Early and high summer, especially hot, dry spells, see most fish activity in the fastest and therefore most oxygenated runs – especially those thick with streamer weed. Almost no water at this time is too shallow, even for large barbel and chub. Stalking visible fish is often very rewarding at this time of year but requires stealth and care.

Autumn Towards the end of summer and into autumn, when showers begin to swell the river, barbel start to feed in earnest in the main stream as they sense the approach of winter. Swimfeeder tackle with hemp as feed and hookbait (use six grains on a hair rig) is a particularly good method at this time of year, changing to legered luncheon meat if the water colours up following a lot of rain.

Winter This season sees most fish move to slower water to conserve energy, but remember this can often be just a depression in the river bed below a fast surface current.

Barbel and bream are the first to be put off feeding by a fall in temperature, but sport in general is usually poor when the temperature is falling. However, all fish seem to sense when a very cold snap is coming and often feed well to build up their energy reserves just before it arrives. The start of a cold spell is the worst time for fishing, with only the odd chub prepared to feed. After a few days of low, stable temperatures most fish apart from barbel and bream gradually begin to feed again.

Back end As soon as water temperatures start to rise – which can be as early as February – the fish react, and by the back end (the last four weeks or so) of the fishing season until March 15, all species can be on the move and feeding.

Fishing fast rivers

Many anglers are wary of fast rivers, often because their attempts have failed. The commonest mistake is fishing too light.

To present a bait properly in heavy flow demands the use of weight; and to hook, hold and land fish in fast, and often weedy, water takes strong rods, lines and hooks. Fish in fast-flowing rivers don't have time to inspect a bait but must grab it immediately before it goes past, so you don't need to use light tackle to tempt bites.

Line strengths should be 5lb – 8lb (2.3 – 3.6kg) for barbel and chub, and 3lb (1.4kg) for roach, dace and perch. Hooks should be forged, in sizes from 16 to 4.

For floatfishing use an Avon rod and Avon and balsa floats carrying from 3AAA to 6SSG. Bulk most of the shot nearer the hook than the float (see below).

For legering you need an Avon quivertip rod, a range of weights from swan shot to 2oz (57g), and a selection of block-end swimfeeders up to 2oz (57g). A simple sliding rig is best.

▼ *This fine net of seven big chub and one roach was the reward for reading a fast-flowing river and using sensible tackle.*

▲ *On an Avon float rig bulk most of the shot nearer the hook than the float. This keeps the bait down near the bottom.*

Avon float

flow →

bulk shot

hook

Slow lowland rivers

The Midlands and south of England feature some fine slow moving rivers. Ken Whitehead finds that – if you're any good at botany – reading the water is easy.

▼ *A wide, slow bend where fish gather in undercut banks makes a good swim, if you conceal yourself. Algae around the bank shows this water is nearly still.*

The lowland rivers of the Midlands and south of England are among the most important of Britain's angling waters. Characteristically they are slow moving and wide, with extremes of depth and masses of bankside vegetation in the warmer months.

Such rivers hold a good head of fish, many reaching specimen – and in some cases record – size. A wide variety of species thrives in slow waters, particularly bream, carp, tench, roach and rudd.

Many other species have adapted themselves to this tranquil habitat, especially chub, pike and perch. Good-sized eels also feature regularly on the big fish list – especially at the estuary end of such waters.

Round the bend

The soft, rich pasture land often found around these rivers is responsible for their winding course. Winter floods cut and undermine soft banks – these then erode and create bends. Holes in the bed are excavated or filled by successive winter floods – meaning the productive life of each swim is often short. You have to be flexible and ready to fish new swims at the start of each season.

It is the lush growth in and around these rivers that provides the key to reading them. The fertile soil encourages the fast growth of water plants and bankside weeds. These produce the prolific insect life that make the fish so big.

All this vegetation makes access to swims difficult – especially at times of droughts or

◄ *A typical early stage of a slow lowland river. Dense bankside vegetation almost chokes the water, especially in summer. Getting to grips with these swims calls for plenty of scrabbling around. Ken Whitehead recommends fishing these areas in the winter, when there is less weed around.*

floods. It's tempting to clear one swim and stay with it. But your success depends entirely on water craft. The angler who fishes just one swim, never reading the water, has little success. The same applies to those who only fish where others have fished before. A good angler needs to try out every rig and tactic in the book if he is to make any worthwhile catches.

A SLOW FLOWING LOWLAND RIVER

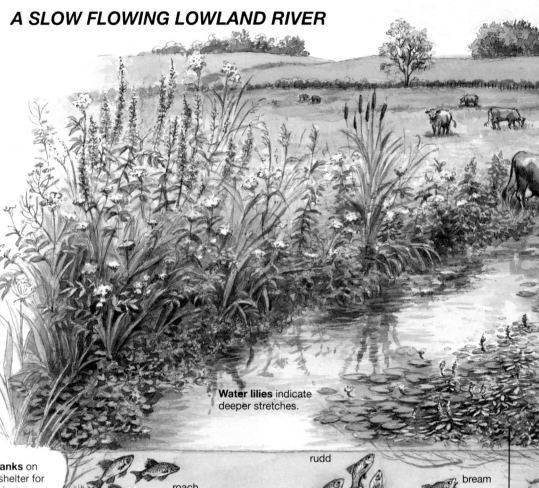

Water lilies indicate deeper stretches.

Undercut banks on bends give shelter for several species.

Silt gathers at the bends, encouraging weeds which give fish shelter.

On wide stretches swims are slower where the water deepens.

roach

rudd

bream

tench

Pondweeds (*Potamogeton* species) show medium depth.

Key weeds

The most important skill is being able to estimate the depth of water between the banks. Learning and remembering the different weeds help here. Reed mace and rushes indicate shallow water. Pondweeds (*Potamogeton*) and Canadian waterweed (*Elodea canadensis*) show deeper water, while lilies surface in water that is deeper still.

Water with no weeds is probably the deepest of all! It is worth immediate attention.

Upper reaches

Slow rivers can be split into three sections. The upper reaches from the source downstream; the main, middle, section; and the tidal reaches.

The upper reaches are narrow and overgrown during summer, with just a trickle of a current. Anglers need to rove around to find the fish, and the places from which they can be reached.

Ken Whitehead uses a long rod. Many

▼ *The Suffolk Stour – a good example of a slow lowland river. The rushes show a shallow bank and yellow water-lilies deeper water.*

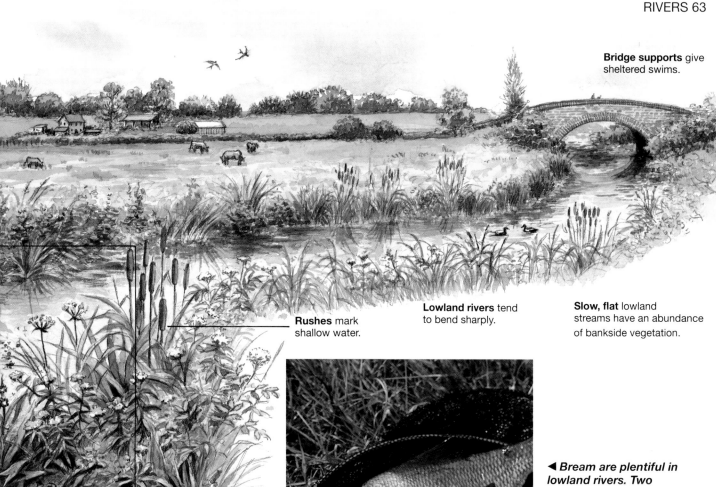

Bridge supports give sheltered swims.

Rushes mark shallow water.

Lowland rivers tend to bend sharply.

Slow, flat lowland streams have an abundance of bankside vegetation.

Cattle drinks are good places for roach sheltering from the faster flow of the main current.

anglers use a short rod on these narrow waters, but a longer rod allows you to keep back from the water's edge and the skyline.

Camouflage or drab clothing is essential. So is light feed that can be spread upstream, or on to water in front of the angler. Maggots are probably best, though many anglers use a light cloud mix, through which a hookbait can be worked.

Freelining is a sure method of success on narrow stretches; so is dapping with floating baits. Keep the hook on the large side and be prepared to bully a hooked fish into the landing net. If you don't you will lose it – and probably every fish along the next swim downstream.

Winter is the best time to get to grips with this section since weed growth is reduced and it becomes possible to long trot when the flow is normal. Try a rolling leger when there is more water than usual. Big baits such as lobworms and large pieces of crust or paste, fished close to the bottom, bring firm bites – and keep small fish from worrying the bait.

Middle stretches

The middle stretches provide extremes in water features. Straight stretches of bank are not only few and far between, but frequently a warning of shallow swims. Here

◄ *Bream are plentiful in lowland rivers. Two hotspots are bends in the river – which give shelter – and holes in the river bed. Locate these with a plummet, groundbait them, and wait for the greedy bream to start biting.*

▼ *A beautiful riverside scene in the Sussex countryside, complete with windmill! The flat landscape and sharply curving banks are typical of lowland rivers. Fish could be gathered in that curve in the bank.*

suspended silt has often dropped to the bottom, leaving a muddy bed that encourages weed growth.

Fish, especially pike, can be holed up among the weed. Watch the weeds for shaking and movement as the fish brush against them. Use freeline tactics, or at least as little weight as possible. A plummet often reveals a deep hole where groundbaiting can collect bottom feeders such as bream in large numbers – particularly over a period of time.

It is at bends in the river, particularly wide, slow ones, that the fish are most likely to be found. The current undercuts banks and forms deep runs and these are often weed-free. The silt has usually been washed down, leaving a firm, clean bottom.

With a steady flow on the water, roach, rudd, bream and excellent chub can be caught in large numbers. Light tackle is essential. You should keep low, tucked down behind any cover growing on or along the side of the water. It is an ideal situation for using the roach pole – feeding little and often. Better fish are generally taken on a very light and accurately cast leger.

Where the river widens

As the river widens the flow tends to slow and – during the summer months – virtually stop. The immediate effect is for weed to take hold, blocking good swims. Some hard work with a good rake in a suitable swim soon clears a space. Groundbait scattered on this patch of open water attracts the fish.

Winter's high water levels and fast currents allow long trotting and legering along the deepest parts. Avoid block-end feeders and other legering aids that create unnecessary splash and disturbance. Search for – and mark – eddies, cattle drinks and sheltered swims behind bridge supports or at the end of root-infested banks. They are natural fish collecting areas and provide sheltered water during floods.

Weirs along the course of lowland rivers supply oxygenated water during drought conditions – always take the opportunity to fish them, perhaps using silkweed, fruitbaits and natural insects. They are the home of big chub which, Ken finds, respond to small spinners and plugs, plastic lures and big artificial flies at any month of the year.

◄ *Roach thrive in slow-flowing rivers. Use light tackle and be prepared to search for the shoals.*

▼ *A typical lowland river seldom flows in a straight line. The soft rich soils they meander through are constantly eroded by the rivers, forming sharp curves and ever-changing swims. Lowland rivers never remain the same.*

Small rivers in summer

The banks of some small rivers are so rich in vegetation they wouldn't look out of place in a jungle. Graham Marsden tells you what you can catch.

More often than not small rivers are full of character. They wind their way through the countryside like sinuous snakes slithering through the grass. Because of this winding – sometimes so severe that the river goes back on itself – the current hits the bends with considerable force. This is especially so during high water.

The current undercuts banks, exposes tree roots and piles debris against overhanging branches. With every thousand gallons of water that pours through, the river's character changes subtly. This is good news for the angler because it means that every swim is like a fingerprint: unique – not another one like it anywhere on the river. This makes for exciting fishing because you can try perhaps half a dozen very different swims within the space of a morning or evening's fishing.

► *Graham unhooks a chub taken from the River Dove. This fish fell to stick float tactics – a versatile method which suits many types of swims on these smaller rivers.*

▼ *Cheshire's River Dane is typical of the small rivers that Graham likes to fish.*
  Here an angler makes use of an island. By positioning himself in the middle of the river he is able to work a bait along the slightly deeper water. It often pays to explore deeper-looking channels, holes, gaps between weed and the water around obstacles such as fallen trees and islands.

► *Here's a really interesting looking swim. Winter floods have scoured away the banks, causing a tree to fall into the river. Flood debris has collected around its base and made a home for chub and barbel. This angler used quivertip tactics to lure a barbel from its hole.*

In weirpools you find several features thrown together. Fast water under the sill is home to barbel. Chub and dace hold the slightly slower water. The slack margins and eddies are where pike and perch ambush their prey.

Tree roots break through the bank and into the river - providing cover for big perch.

An island splits the current. In the fast water to one side you may find grayling and trout.

Below the island streamer weed has managed to establish itself in the fast water. Barbel hide in gravel channels between the weed.

A deep hole has been scoured out where the current hits the bank. This is home to a shoal of big chub.

A glide – where the water slows slightly - is a gathering place for shoals of roach and dace.

What you'll find

You can find a wealth of different species in small rivers: roach, perch, pike, chub, dace, barbel and, in the cleaner rivers, even trout and grayling. But it is a mistake to think that because a river is small the fish are small. Far from it – most small rivers are capable of producing fish at least equal to, if not bigger than, those found in larger rivers.

Get to know your river

The best way of becoming a competent small river angler is to get to know the river as intimately as you can. Speaking to other anglers is a start, but there really is no substitute for walking along the river bank and fishing it at every single opportunity.

One of the essential features of these small rivers is that when the water is low and clear you can often see the fish – some-thing that you can't usually do on larger coloured rivers. With the aid of polarizing glasses you can spot fish and even identify them if you can creep up close enough.

When you are not actually fishing but merely rambling along the bank it is perhaps more important to pay attention to features rather than fish. Make a note of where the weed beds and other snags and likely fish-holding areas are – where the water deepens, if it runs over sand, gravel, or silt, for example.

This kind of knowledge stands you in good stead when the water is slightly high and coloured. These conditions can produce the best sport but they hide many of the features visible under normal conditions and make fish spotting impossible.

There is nothing worse than fishing an unfamiliar river when it is high. Coloured water makes it difficult to tell the difference between deep and shallow water without plumbing, and to some extent you have to fish blind.

Every swim imaginable

Every type of river swim you can imagine can be found on a small river and countless varieties of each type of swim.

Deep holes and glides on the outsides of bends are very common. Here you find roach, perch, dace and chub. Lurking not far away – usually in the slack water on the inside of the bend – you'll find pike on the lookout for an easy meal. Many of these deeper holes have trees and bushes on the outside of the bends. Their roots strengthen the banks, allowing the current to undercut them deeply without the bank collapsing. This is where the bigger chub live.

Fast, shallow water is always worth

Where to fish

There are a great many small rivers but here are a few of the best.
- **Berkshire,** River Kennet.
- **Cheshire,** River Dane.
- **North Yorkshire,** Rivers Nidd and Swale.
- **Oxfordshire,** Rivers Cherwell and Windrush.
- **Warwickshire,** River Teme.

Tip *A cautious approach*

Remember that as easily as you can spot fish on a small river, they can spot you. Stealth, then, is the key word.

Tackle up well away from the bank and off the skyline. Approach swims using every bit of cover available. Keep low – even crawling on all fours when necessary. It's a good idea to wear dark colours.

▼ *Swimfeeder tactics are great on weirpools. On other parts of the river – where you want to roll a bait across glides under rafts and into undercuts – a simple SSG shot link leger is best. Baits such as worms, cheese, bread, slugs and casters are best.*

In the slower water roach and dace make an easier prey for pike and perch hiding among marginal weed.

A SMALL RIVER IN SUMMER

◄ *This angler looks suitably pleased with this 7lb (3.2kg) barbel taken from a small weirpool on the River Kennet. The barbel's large fins and streamlined shape make it a tremendously hard fighter.*

Tip Wild rover approach

There are two good reasons why it pays to adopt a roving approach on small rivers. First, although some swims do hold shoals, many hold only a few large fish. So once you have taken two or three fish it isn't worth hanging around if you are no longer getting bites.

Secondly, the fish are easily scared and often move themselves.

fishing in summer, for here the water is well-oxygenated and weedy, offering the cover fish need so as not to be exposed to predators. This is a favourite haunt of barbel.

Where willows and other trees overhang, trailing their branches on the water's surface, debris collects – twigs, branches, dead weed, leaves and anything else that floats down the river (especially during high water) – forming a raft that becomes a roof over the heads of fish. Chub are very fond of these places. Floating crust fished tight up against these rafts of rubbish is well worth a try – especially on summer evenings.

Where the current leaves a bend it often forms a glide that gradually shallows to faster water below. These glides are good for roach and chub. Where the river bed rises – just before the faster water – is often a winner for dace.

Weirpools are excellent in summer for all species. This is because water tumbling over the sill drives oxygen into what might otherwise be stale water.

Directly under the sill you'll find barbel, while in the calmer water below are chub and roach. Pike and perch inhabit the slacker eddies at the sides of the pool but they are quite willing to venture into faster water to seek prey if no prey has come to them. Dace are to be found in the faster water as it leaves the pool.

How to catch them

Although many small rivers respond well to the light-line, small-hook approach, there are plenty that give up their best fish to a heavier, bigger bait style.

One favourite method for summer chub on small rivers is a simple, free-lined slug on a size 4 hook to 5lb (2.26kg) b.s. line. Sneak up to the river and spot your chub, then cast a little upstream of it so that the slug tumbles past it. Strike when you see the gills flare and the slug disappear. The same technique with a large lobworm is good too – for both chub and barbel.

▼ *Three fine dace may not be everyone's idea of a bumper morning's catch but on light tackle dace give a good account of themselves. On a warm summer evening dace and chub are quite partial to a dry fly.*

Large coloured rivers

Rain-fed rivers that turn a ruddy brown when in flood are sometimes called coloured rivers. Notable examples include the Severn, the Great Ouse and the Trent. Graham Marsden reveals the secrets of fishing these waters.

A large coloured river is one that is rain-fed and becomes the colour of stewed tea when in the height of flood.

Apart from the Severn, Trent and Great Ouse, other popular large coloured rivers are the Thames, the Wye in Wales, and the Ribble, Swale and Ouse in the north.

Rain-fed rivers never run with the same sparkling clarity of chalk streams such as the Hampshire Avon or Dorset Stour. Even when no rain has fallen for some time there is always an undertone of green, grey or brown, subtle as it may be.

This colouring can be an advantage to the angler because his movements on the bank are not as obvious to the fish. This means they won't scare so easily. But the colouring can also be a disadvantage because, by the same token, the fish are not so easily seen – choosing a good swim becomes more of an educated guess.

All the usual coarse species are present in large coloured rivers. These include dace, roach, chub, bream, barbel, pike and perch in the middle and lower reaches. Brown trout and grayling can be found in the upper reaches of some rain-fed rivers, and

the mighty salmon will run nearly the length of the river – from the sea virtually to the source.

Varying nature

The upper reaches of these rivers are narrower, with faster, shallower, water that winds its way through the hills. Any trout or grayling present inhabit the fast water, while coarse fish living in these sections seek out the slow glides and the deeper

▲ *Graham Marsden is a well-known angler and broadcaster. He is author of several books on fishing and acknowledged to be a leading authority on bream.*

◀ *The Trent is a typical rain-fed river, wide and coloured. Such rivers often have steep banks in their lower reaches, caused by the volume of floodwater – and wading can be a good tactic.*

▼ *This view of the Thames near Oxford shows clearly that there is always a hint of colouring in large rain-fed rivers. Even during a drought silt is always present in the water.*

pools on the bends.

The middle and lower reaches are generally wider and deeper. The river does not wind as much, and there are high banks and deep undercuts where surging flood-water has gouged the soil. As the river nears the sea an increasing number of tributaries join it. Heavy rain has a greater effect in these stretches as the tributaries fill the mother river with heavily silted coloured water. There are times when fishing becomes impossible.

Finding the fish

When the river is flowing at its normal level there are certain things to look for in choosing a swim, according to which species you wish to catch.

Roach prefer smooth glides 4-6ft (1.2-1.8m) deep, that meander beneath the bushes overhanging the river's edge. Hawthorn and elder bushes seem especially attractive to roach – years ago elderberries were a popular roach bait.

Dace like a slightly faster current, particularly where it shelves up from the deeper to shallower water, just before it breaks up and tumbles rapidly.

Perch love slacks on the inside of bends, where they can chase the minnows. Pike are also partial to such swims, but they are not averse to hunting in faster water if their prey can be found there.

Barbel are very fond of weed. They like to lurk in strong-flowing – but not too fast – water, over clean gravel. Wherever you find a snag, such as a sunken tree branch or a boulder, you can generally find barbel. In the warmer months, smaller barbel are also found in numbers in the shallow, fast, weedy lengths.

Chub favour water of medium pace, specially where there is a 'crease' that divides the current from the slack water at the edge. Rubbish rafts, too, are among their favourite haunts. These are accumulations of debris collecting around an overhanging tree branch trailing in the water. In fact chub love anything that provides a roof over their heads, be it a raft, an undercut bank, a

▲ *A barbel caught on a swimfeeder on the Severn. Swimfeedering with smelly baits greatly improves the chances of the fish finding your hookbait in coloured rivers.*

On the spot

Using a swimfeeder is the best method when fishing heavily coloured water. But you are wasting your time if you don't cast to the same spot every feed.

Pick out a marker on the opposite bank, such as a tree. Every time you cast, aim for the marker. You only want one trail – to your hook!

Elder and hawthorn bushes on the bank are attractive to some species of fish. In season, many fish eat elderberries which drop into the water.

Chub are especially fond of waiting for tasty morsels under a raft of debris caught in the overhanging branches of a tree.

raft of debris

A SPLASH OF COLOUR

Undercut banks, usually on the outsides of bends, provide shelter for chub out of the main flow from where they can intercept food carried down in the current. Tree roots make this shelter even more attractive.

chub

chub

Showing its true colours

It is when rain-fed rivers are in flood that they reveal their true colours. This is the River Thames in flood, at Wytham near Oxford. Where tributaries merge with main rivers some interesting hotspots occur. The main river backs up the tributary, forming a slack. Such slacks provide a welcome break for a wide variety of fish struggling against the rapid floodwater.

thick weedbed, or a tunnel of weeping willow.

Bream thrive in the deep, slow, lower reaches of a river – where the river bed is mainly mud or silt.

High waters

It is in times of flood that waters such as the Severn and the Ouse really live up to their label of large coloured rivers. The increased water and disturbed silt give them an unmistakable character. Where tributaries meet the main river excellent swims form during times of high water. The main river backs up the tributary, forming a slack in

▶ *The Thames between Culham and Abingdon, showing its coloured tint. Boats help to stir up the rich sediment at the bottom of such rivers. In busy boating waters fish tend to stay nearer the bank. They are found in the middle of the river from the end of the boating season.*

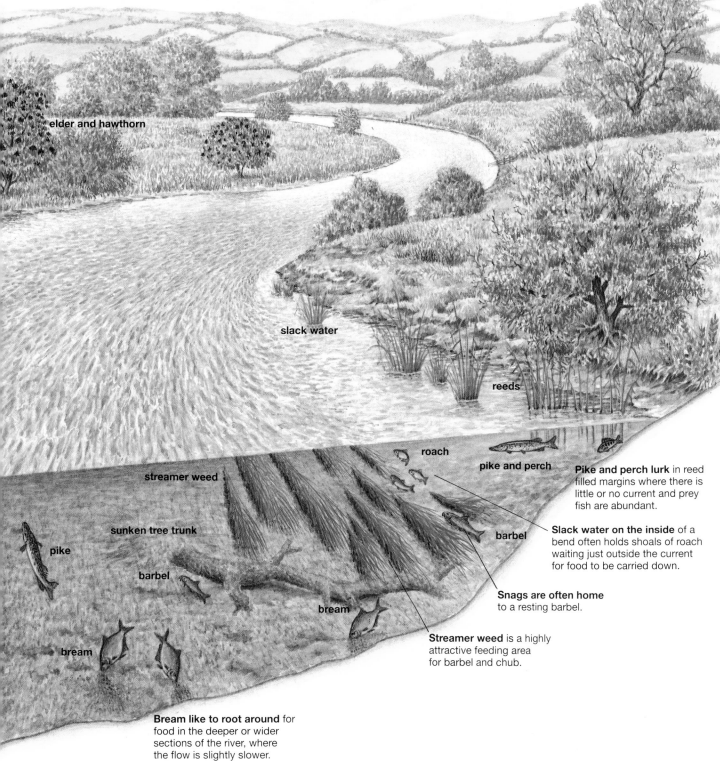

elder and hawthorn

slack water

reeds

roach

pike and perch

streamer weed

sunken tree trunk

pike

barbel

barbel

bream

bream

bream

Pike and perch lurk in reed filled margins where there is little or no current and prey fish are abundant.

Slack water on the inside of a bend often holds shoals of roach waiting just outside the current for food to be carried down.

Snags are often home to a resting barbel.

Streamer weed is a highly attractive feeding area for barbel and chub.

Bream like to root around for food in the deeper or wider sections of the river, where the flow is slightly slower.

▲ *The Severn clearly shows some typical characteristics of a large coloured river. It is wide and features high banks on the far side. Try legering with a swimfeeder.*

which many fish take refuge. Close to the bank at such hotspots – among the reeds and rushes where sediment usually builds up – predators like pike lie in wait. During severe flooding such retreats are used by both the hunters and the hunted. All the species can be found holed up together because their normal swims are under threat.

Where one river is joined by a slower-flowing river, which frequently happens to coloured rivers as they near the sea, an eddy forms. The swirling water carves out a depression, which bottom feeding species appreciate.

Fishing rain-fed rivers

Smelly baits, such as cheese and luncheon meat, are effective when the water is coloured. They are easier to detect at times when the currents have disturbed the sediment and the fish have to rely on smell rather than sight.

One non-smelly bait, a large lobworm, also proves very effective in coloured water.

There are various different methods of fishing coloured rivers. One is trotting with a stick float. This method, using maggot or caster as bait, catches all species, but it is particularly good for such fish as dace, roach and chub.

When fishing a crease, or a glide, of slow or medium-paced water within two rod lengths of the bank, a stick float can be unbeatable, but remember to feed regularly.

A swimfeeder, packed with hemp and caster, is effective for barbel. Don't be afraid to use a really heavy feeder so that you can hold the bottom in the centre of the river. Cast and feed regularly.

Night chubbing

Yet another excellent way of chub fishing large rain-fed rivers is to visit the water an hour or so before darkness, when most other anglers are packing up.

Tackle up a quivertip rod with a simple leger rig, then wander along the bank, using bread crust or paste, luncheon meat or cheese. It's rare that chub won't feed at this time. Bites are usually very positive, even when you are using tackle heavy enough to land fish through snags. The best time to fish is during the three or four hours from dusk. The idea is to catch one or two fish from one swim, and then move on to the next.

▼ *Fishing a large coloured river is not all green river banks in summer sunshine. This is a very wintry view of the Yorkshire Ouse at Lendal Bridge in York. In winter fish slower swims.*

A small fast river in winter

Top angling writer John Bailey loves fishing small rivers in winter. If you see him crawling on hands and knees don't worry – these are his special fishing tactics!

England is riddled with small streams that are easily overlooked. Yet, says John Bailey, they offer good fishing all year round and, in winter especially, can be really dynamite.

It is true to say that small, fast flowing rivers can provide fishing in the most atrocious weather conditions. Even when there's not a ghost of a chance elsewhere these waters can be productive.

Whether there are floods or shivering hard frost, rapid streams yield chub and dace, often with grayling and roach, and sometimes decent pike and perch. But you need to keep quiet and low!

A good read

One beauty of the small river is that it is easy to read. Even in the bleak mid-winter, when frosty winds moan, the swims scream for your attention. Once you have found them, the swims are so small you know fish won't be far away.

Any mill or weir pool is worth immediate investigation. The extra depth gives fish security in low, clear water and in floods offers protection from the full force of the current.

Such a friendly environment encourages a lot of fish to remain in the pool throughout the winter, and it is rare that you leave such

▼ *Sharp bends on small fast rivers are good places for roach and chub. The depth increases on some bends, causing the water flow to steady. Roach welcome the respite. This angler is roaching on light tackle.*

▲ *Chubbing on small rivers can be very productive in winter. Legering in deep holes under river banks is often successful.*

a place completely biteless.

Almost as attractive are the sharper bends where the depth increases and the flow steadies a little. Chub and roach like these bend swims particularly, and grayling are found there too when the winter weather is very bitter.

Any snags, such as fallen branches, make the swim even better. Always remember that in small rivers, fish feel very vulnerable and flock to any feature that provides cover and an illusion of sanctuary.

Narrow thoughts

Often small rivers narrow dramatically and where the banks come closer together a stretch of deep water is produced. Roach, grayling and the bigger dace love these areas – especially if the current steadies up a little.

Average sized dace generally congregate a little lower down where the water shallows and speeds up again. Good nets of 4-6oz (113-170g) fish can be amassed quickly until the shoal takes fright.

The only trouble is that native brown trout often share these swims – and catching them so soon after they have spawned can do them harm. If you catch one, put it back into the water at once.

Keep on moving

Since different species like varying areas, they are not all going to flock to your swim. You need to go and find them.

Small islands, ditches or dyke inflows, moored boats – in short, anything out of the

IN THE BLEAK MID-WINTER

Branches provide excellent cover for lurking pike.

Worms are often a killing bait on a small river. On very difficult, cold days, a tiny red worm tipped with a single maggot can produce a result where other baits fail.

▶ *Trotting for grayling on a Kennet tributary. Fish – especially grayling – are often found where rivers narrow and deepen, and the water slackens in pace.*

Just the stuff for pike

Small rivers often hold a decent head of pike. Again, it pays to travel light and try a good many swims with a small, twitched deadbait.

If a pike is in residence it is likely to take at once. The take is often vicious, causing quite a swirl in the water. Strike at once and be prepared for a good fight. John once saw a 21lb (9.4kg) female come from a swim that was only 1.8m (6ft) wide and 60cm (2ft) deep!

In winter pike are often bigger – in spawning condition – and they are in better shape than summer pike.

Spinning won't work as well in the winter, because the extra water brings cloudy soil which decreases the pike's field of vision.

A good, smelly, deadbait is far more detectable because cloudy waters won't obscure the smell. Try a mackerel, cut in half to release the juices. Remember to keep well concealed.

ordinary – can attract the various small river fish stocks.

This is why it pays dividends to keep mobile on these streams. Make sure your gear is light and portable and visit as many likely looking swims as possible.

Be prepared to walk miles in a day and give each likely looking swim ten to fifteen minutes before moving on again.

In small swims, bites are generally pretty immediate and there is little point in trying to build a swim up if the fish are hundreds of yards away. A chub, in particular, often

takes a bait the moment it hits the water – provided it hasn't been disturbed in any way.

Special tactics

Your approach to a small river swim is, therefore, absolutely crucial – especially when the water runs low and clear.

It pays to walk slowly and carefully, and to keep well away from the bank. Also make sure your shadow never falls on the water. It looks stupid, but John always moves into the swim on his hands and knees. He never

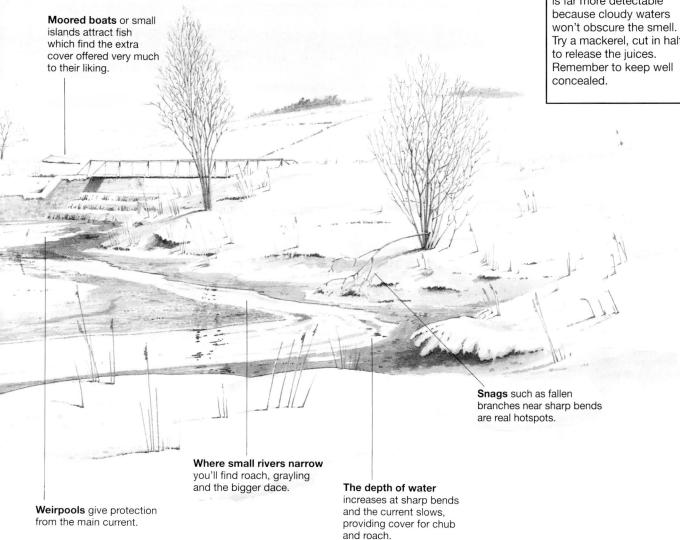

Moored boats or small islands attract fish which find the extra cover offered very much to their liking.

Snags such as fallen branches near sharp bends are real hotspots.

Where small rivers narrow you'll find roach, grayling and the bigger dace.

The depth of water increases at sharp bends and the current slows, providing cover for chub and roach.

Weirpools give protection from the main current.

sits on a box either, preferring a cushion, or a piece of plastic sheeting, that gives him a much lower profile against the bank.

Hustle a hooked fish from the swim as quickly as possible – leave it for too long and it scares all the fish in a small, shallow piece of water. This type of fishing demands great physical and mental awareness – so keep alert.

Selecting baits

Without doubt, the most likely method to catch on a small river is the trotted maggot. The perfect combination is a 12ft (3.6m) match rod, 3lb (1.4kg) main line, 2lb (0.9kg) hooklength and a light float, set to trip one or two maggots on a size 18 hook along the bottom.

Dace, roach and grayling all fall for this approach. You can spend a bit of time building up the swim, introducing just half a dozen free feed maggots into the water each cast.

▶ *A winter scene, such as this, might – at first – look bad for fishing. But look again and you can see a number of snags and shallower areas that offer cover for fish.*

In very cold weather – when day-time temperatures rarely creep above freezing – a bait fished hard on the bottom is often preferable.

A sensitive quivertip, a tiny swimfeeder and a single maggot on a size 18 hook often prove necessary to entice fish in these Arctic conditions.

Open the flood baits

When the weather swings and the river floods, then larger baits can be used. Three maggots on a size 14 hook, or a piece of breadflake on a size 12, should take all the small river species. If the water is really coloured, leger them hard on the bottom, just out of the main current – in an eddy, or behind a fallen branch. Meat, worms and cheese – all flavourful baits – also do well in these conditions.

A river that is settling down after a flood offers the best possible chance of a really notable fish. Choose a slow, deeper swim and settle in this an hour before darkness. Feed in two or three slices of mashed bread and then, as the light fades, leger a good sized piece of flake on a size 10 hook. You might have to wait a while for a bite, but when it comes, it is very positive – and an excellent roach, chub or dace could well be the result.

If there are any present, you can even hope for a stray barbel to set the cold night alight.

◀ *A brace of chub and somehow it's all worthwhile! People often gape in amazement when they see anglers fishing in Siberian conditions – but look what you can catch!*

The challenge of weirpools

The combination of rushing water, quiet eddies and swirling undercurrents, which between them are home to numerous species – including barbel, bream and eels – makes weirpools exciting places to fish.

Weirs are man-made structures that regulate river flow. Although they vary from simple walls to complicated designs with several sluice gates, they all have certain features in common. The powerful currents that tear at the river bed create a range of habitats from the boiling cauldron at the outfall to the quiet stretches of water at the sides.

The white water of the outfall is too turbulent for all but the occasional hardy brown trout, while further on the fast flow is ideally suited to streamlined dace.

By contrast the quieter eddies and backwaters are the favoured haunts of browsing bream and of pike lying in wait to ambush their prey.

Between these extremes, the steady flows of water play host to a mixed brew of fish, all competing for the food washed into the weir from the main riverway.

Reading the water

All stretches of water, from a pond to a river, have surface clues that provide a detailed map to the hidden world below. Being able to read the map is part and parcel of catching fish – the better your 'water craft' the better your catches will be. The weirpool angler must look at the surface clues held in the current and try to visualize what is going on below.

The bed: you'll need to know what's on the weirpool bed to have an idea what sort of fish you can find there. For instance, a fine, soft surface will encourage the bottom-

▼ *An angler prepares to cast a swimfeeder into the basin of Diglis Weir on the River Severn in Worcester, in search of summer barbel and bream. Diglis Weir, which holds large stocks of roach, dace, chub and pike as well, is one of many weirpools around the country that can be fished on a day ticket.*

feeding bream, while barbel and roach are known to favour gravel.

Surface boiling indicates boulders or other large obstructions. The faster the current, the larger the obstruction on the weirpool bed. The slowest currents allow sand and mud to be deposited, the fastest only large rocks and boulders.

To find out what's at the bottom, drag a leger across the bed to see what it's made of – sand, gravel, stones or rocks. Plumb the depth to identify runs, ledges and hollows.

Undercurrents: you also need a picture of the lower currents. Those on the surface can be misleading, as the slower water below may move in the opposite direction and any loose feeding may be well off the mark.

◀ *This 7½lb (3.4kg) barbel came from the Kennet. Barbel are a favourite quarry of the weirpool angler and a fish that demands strong gear.*

Weirpools: where to find the fish

The table below lists the fish commonly found in weirpools, together with their likely locations at normal water levels and recommended baits and techniques. The information here applies to a typical weirpool and will, of course, vary from place to place. Remember that in raging floods all fish may seek shelter in the eddies and backwaters.

Fish	Location	Best techniques
Barbel	Basin, tail, run-off, fastish eddies	Legering luncheon meat and lobworms; swimfeedering maggots, casters and hemp; trotting maggots and sweetcorn
Bream	Basin, eddies, backwaters	Swimfeedering maggots, casters, redworms, breadflake and sweetcorn
Chub	Basin, tail, run-off, eddies	Trotting and legering breadflake, luncheon meat, cheese, small deadbaits, lobworms and sweetcorn; floating crust; small spoons, spinners and plugs
Dace	Race, tail, run-off	Trotting maggots and casters
Eels	Basin, eddies, backwaters	Legering lobworms and small deadbaits
Grayling	Tail, run-off	Trotting maggots
Perch	Basin, tail, eddies, backwaters	Trotting and legering lobworms and small fish; small spoons, spinners and plugs
Pike	Eddies, backwaters	Spoons, spinners and plugs; trotting and legering deadbaits
Roach	Tail, run-off, eddies, backwaters	Trotting and legering breadflake, sweetcorn, maggots and casters; trotting hemp
Brown trout	Outfall, race, tail, run-off	Small spoons, spinners and plugs; roll-legering lobworms – trout licence needed

Weirs vary in size and complexity of design but all have a number of features in common. Each part of the weirpool has its own type of flow and particular river bed. These determine the kind of fish that live there and the best techniques to use when fishing them (see chart, left).

backwater

run-off

Use a heavy balsa float with the shot bulked near the hook to beat the surface currents and show if the lower currents are pulling in a different direction.

Fishing the weirpool

Weirpool fish can grow to very large sizes, so don't use too fine tackle. For example, hooking a large barbel in fast water requires line of about 10lb (4.5kg) breaking strain, with a strong rod and forged hook to match. Weirpool pike are also tremendous fighters and put their stillwater cousins to shame.

Lightish gear can be used at the tail and run-off but you'll be in trouble if your fish sets off up the race.

One of the most productive areas of the weirpool is the tail. Regular feeding here can draw fish from the eddies and basin. These areas usually have a clean gravel bottom, giving you a choice of leger, swimfeeder or float. A great day's fishing can be had by trotting maggots or sweetcorn during the day then swimfeedering maggots for an hour or two at dusk. All manner of fish can be caught this way. If the current over the tail

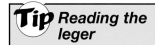

Tip Reading the leger

Drag a leger across the bottom of the weirpool to determine the nature of the river bed. It will:

● Bump and jerk across rocks and boulders
● Grate across stones and gravel
● Catch occasionally in weed
● Pass easily across sand and silt
● Drag heavily but smoothly through mud

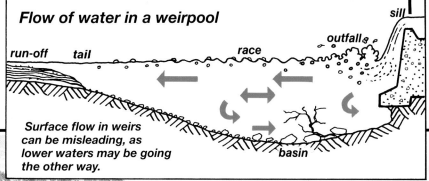

Flow of water in a weirpool

sill
outfall
run-off   tail   race
Surface flow in weirs can be misleading, as lower waters may be going the other way.
basin

eddy
sill
outfall
race
basin
tail
eddy

◄ *The weirpools of the lower Thames are huge. Shown here is Teddington Weir, which marks the upper limit of the tidal river and is host to big shoals of roach, dace and bream.*

is turbulent you'll need a chunky balsa float taking several swan shot. In smoother currents use a stick float.

If you are lucky enough to have the weirpool to yourself you can rove it with a rolling leger and fish from any number of different points. Use a main line of 8lb (3.5kg) and have 6lb (2.7kg) and 3lb (1.4kg) hooklength line with you. Take a range of baits such as lobworms, cheese, luncheon meat, breadflake and sweetcorn. Finally, if you have a selection of leger weights from ⅛oz (3.5g) to 1½oz (42.5g) with you, you are set up to catch every type of fish in the pool except pike – and even they will occasionally take lobworms. Bites will vary from the rod-slamming takes of barbel to the gentle plucks of wary chub.

Night fishing, if allowed, can be productive – particularly for barbel and eels. Barbel respond to luncheon meat legered in the tail and run-off. A small deadbait legered in an eddy or in the basin may tempt a big eel.

Tip Best time to fish

During the summer and autumn months and in dry spells in winter all areas of a weirpool can usually be fished. In high summer, when the main river is low, weirpool fishing is particularly rewarding. The highly oxygenated water attracts fish from the staler water downstream. In winter floods, however, it is often only eddies and backwaters that are fishable.

Where to fish: a selection of the best weirpools

Barbel specialist **Andy Orme** says: over the years I have fished many exciting weirpools. Some of my favourites are:

● The **Royalty** weirpool on the Hampshire Avon is home to some huge barbel and chub, and produces to heavily fed maggot tactics. For permits contact the West Hants Water Company, Knapp Mill, Mill Road, Christchurch, Dorset BH23 2LU (Tel. 0202-499 000).

● The run-off of the weirpool at **Throop** on the nearby Dorset Stour has some great gravel runs between streamer weed that are packed with chub and barbel. Permits are available from The Manager, South Lodge, Holdenhurst Village, Bournemouth, Dorset, BH8 0EF (Tel. 0202-395 532).

● **Aldermaston** weirpool on the Kennet in Berkshire has some superb roach, dace, barbel and chub fishing. For permits contact the Old Mill, Aldermaston, Berkshire RG7 4LB (Tel. 0734-712365).

● The **Kings Weir** fishery on the Lea in Hertfordshire is famous for big catches of chub and barbel.
Season tickets can be obtained by writing to: National Rivers Authority, Thames Region, P.O. Box 214, Reading, Berkshire RG1 8HQ.

● **Diglis Weir** in Worcester on the Severn holds good stocks of many species including pike, barbel, chub, dace, bream, roach, trout and salmon. Day tickets are available from Alan's Tackle Shop, 26 Malvern Road, St. John's, Worcester, WR2 4RU (Tel. 0905-422 107).

● **Tewkesbury Weir** on the Severn in Gloucestershire is only open for coarse fishing between October 1st and January 2nd due to the salmon season.
Below the lock, however, is the lock cutting which is packed with chub, bream, roach and very big pike. Barbel tend to stay in the weirpool. Here normal open/ close season times are applicable. Day tickets can be bought from: The Lockmaster, Upper Lode Lock, Forthampton, Gloucestershire, GL19 4RF (Tel. 0684-293138).

● The many weirpools on the **Thames** are well worth exploring. Smaller upper Thames weirpools are a delight to fish and contain many big specimens including barbel, perch and pike. The weirpools on the lower river are massive and contain some huge shoals of fish. On the Thames you can fish all the following 18 weirpools with just one permit: Grafton, Radcot, Rushey, Shifford, Eynsham, Sandford, Clifton, Goring, Shiplake, Marsh, Hambledon, Hurley, Marlow, Bray, Bell, Shepperton, Sunbury and Molesey. For this superb value for money permit, contact the National Rivers Authority, Thames Region, P.O. Box 214, Reading, Berkshire RG1 8HQ.

There are many other weirpools dotted throughout England that provide very good fishing. Indeed, far too many to list here.
Each regional water authority has details on the whereabouts of these and can tell you where to obtain permits and what type of fish you're likely to catch.

Ireland
Although there are no barbel or chub in the Republic of Ireland, the weirpools scattered throughout the country provide excellent fishing for many other species, notably pike, perch, bream and trout.

River boatyards and marinas

Bill Rushmer investigates waters where the boats are berthed and finds the fishing action runs hot and cold. The hurly-burly of the holiday season is a bit much for the fish, which prefer marinas as a winter home.

Boatyards and marinas are the garages, workshops and termini of the boating fraternity. To the fish that inhabit their waters, they are more like a staff canteen – offering warmth, food and shelter among the traffic and activity of boat enthusiasts and bargees. They can provide terrific sport for the angler who selects his moment and attends to the likely spots in this changeable environment.

▲ *A filter-bed converted into a marina – streamline your tactics by considering the construction and maturity of the venue.*

Seasonal boatyards

Boatyards consist of channels, jetties and buildings close to a river where boats moor up for repairs and construction work. Some features here are fish holders but you have to take care in your approach.

In summer these are very busy places. The activity tends to scare any fish away from the area during the day. Anglers get a cold reception from owners, who often do their best to discourage fishing in the yards.

Even in the night or early morning you might be better off giving other parts of the river your attention.

◄ *If you can get right in among the boatyard structures without upsetting anyone, you could tap in to shoals of fish seeking shelter.*

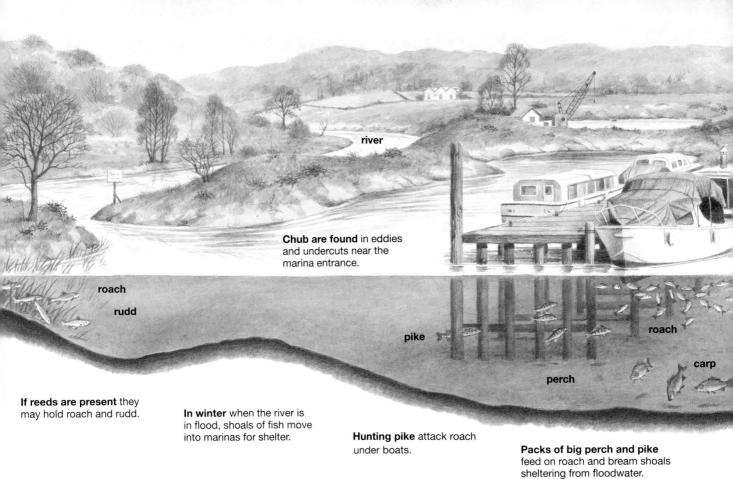

river

Chub are found in eddies and undercuts near the marina entrance.

roach

rudd

pike

roach

perch

carp

If reeds are present they may hold roach and rudd.

In winter when the river is in flood, shoals of fish move into marinas for shelter.

Hunting pike attack roach under boats.

Packs of big perch and pike feed on roach and bream shoals sheltering from floodwater.

A MARINA IN WINTER

▼ *When the boatyard is inactive you might be able to get closer to the fishy features.*
Before you start any serious fishing in marinas or boatyards, check for currents governed by the strength of flow in the adjoining river.

In winter fishing in boatyards is a completely different story. At this time of year the river often floods and the fish move in to boatyards seeking shelter.

Because of the boat activity, which stirs up silt and hinders light penetration, there generally isn't much weed in boatyards either in summer or winter. Roach, dace and chub congregate instead underneath unused boats which provide the protection and cover normally offered by weed.

Houseboats are particularly worthy of the angler's attention as the warmth generated by them attracts large shoals of good roach and other species. Often scraps of food accumulate in the water around houseboats and create an appealing broth which draws the fish. Look for smoke signals coming out of the chimney – but take care not to invade anyone's privacy.

MARINE SERVICES

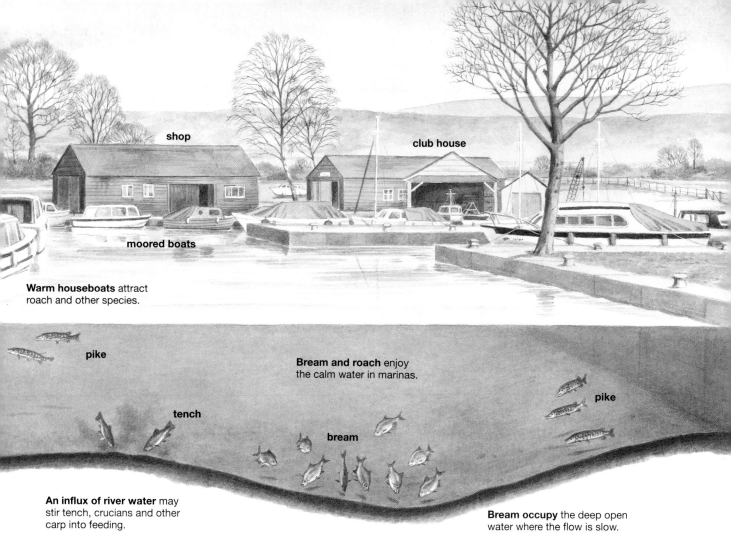

shop

club house

moored boats

Warm houseboats attract
roach and other species.

pike

tench

Bream and roach enjoy
the calm water in marinas.

pike

bream

An influx of river water may
stir tench, crucians and other
carp into feeding.

Bream occupy the deep open
water where the flow is slow.

Not-so-ancient marinas

A marina is basically a harbour for yachts and pleasure boats. Most modern inshore marinas are made by joining a lake or still water to the main river by a comparatively narrow entrance. Boats are taken off the main river through the deep narrow entrance to be moored in the safety of the marina's deep, calm waters.

As boating has increased in popularity there has been a subsequent increase in demand for marina mooring. More and more marinas appear every year as businessmen jump on the bandwagon. They buy up lakes and gravel pits close to rivers, with the long-term aim of obtaining planning permission to breach the bank to produce yet another cheap marina. This avoids the cost of excavating from scratch and appears to be the trend for future developments on many river systems.

Once the bank is breached the building of club houses and similar facilities starts. The banks near the buildings are often concreted and fully developed while the banks farther away from the expensive facilities are often left in their natural state.

The manner in which a marina is constructed has certain implications for the angler. If it is formed from a mature gravel pit then it will hold a stock of fish from the original pit. But if it is completely artificially produced then no natural gravel pit stocks will be present. This is the reason why some marinas hold large stocks of

tench while others hold only natural river species.

There are usually a lot of valuable boats and equipment around marinas, so fishing is often restricted for security reasons.

Areas containing facilities for boat owners with access to the boats are generally kept out of bounds for anglers. Where fishing is allowed it is generally confined to the banks that are clear of boats.

▼*Wherever moored boats offer shelter, fish are likely to move in, closely followed by anglers – en masse in this case.*

High season hidey-holes

Marinas in summer can be very busy places with boats coming and going and clouding up the water – which makes them dirtier than other comparable still waters.

The best angling results in summer are when the boats are not moving. Between dusk and dawn the fish tend to move from their daytime hiding areas in bankside reeds and under banks and disused boats to feed in the main area of the marina.

The species you catch again depend on the water's history. Marinas formed from mature still waters tend to produce more and better lake species such as tench, bream and carp. These species are particularly prone to grazing between dusk and dawn in the deeper open navigable part of the marina. However, once the boat traffic really starts they soon disappear to their hiding places.

Smaller species such as roach, skimmers and rudd tend to feed well during the day-

▲ Shepperton marina on the River Thames – a busy river with increasing angling potential. Judging from sightings in marinas during the summer months it is only a matter of time before a Thames marina produces a carp approaching 40lb (18kg).

▼ In flood conditions when the pace of the river increases, chub, such as this specimen, welcome the calmer water of marinas. At times pike, perch, roach, carp, tench and bream may all be found in marinas.

light hours in shallower water near reeds, weeds or obstructions. Sometimes carp can be seen in similar areas and in lily beds. Large carp are a common sight in many Thames marinas as they bask in the sun away from the boat traffic during the heat of the day.

Many marinas also hold a head of pike and large perch which lie in ambush for their prey species at any suitable point. Sometimes marinas contain unusual features such as dumped cars, which are a bonus snaggy point of attack for predators.

Wintry abundance

In a winter flood marinas can offer some of the most productive fishing in the river system as fish shoal up in the marina seeking shelter from the fierce currents of the river. The marina tends to colour up like the main river, but the parts farther away from the river are often not so highly coloured – which makes fishing much easier.

Again, the fish tend to shoal up in marinas under unused boats that offer shelter. Unlike the boatyard the water is calmer and attracts more bream and roach. Sometimes natural still water species such as tench, crucians and other carp are stirred up into a feeding frenzy by the influx of river water.

In floods chub are also found in marinas. Normally they congregate near the mouth of the marina, in snaggy sheltered spots. In a severe flood they can be present in great numbers.

Once the colour begins to fade the big perch and pike start to hunt in packs, feeding on the large shoals of roach and bream sheltering from the turbulent waters of the river. Where there is a good head of bream the pike can grow to specimen proportions. Big perch on the other hand thrive on the supply of small roach.

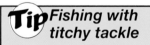
Tip Fishing with titchy tackle

There are many boatyards and marinas along the major rivers all around the country. See what's available on your local river then find out what parts are open to anglers and give them a try. You can often locate the hotspots by watching where other anglers fish.

Always take a short rod to fish the confined spaces between boats. A short quivertip rod is excellent for this type of fishing – its spliced tip cushions the strike and takes the sting out of the lunges of a good fish.

The Norfolk Broads in summer

Famous for their fishing, the Broads may not be what they were but you can still find good sport. John Bailey is your guide.

In the Middle Ages vast amounts of peat were dug for fuel in north-east Norfolk. Gradually the extensive workings flooded to form a network of reed-fringed meres, dykes and slow-moving rivers draining into the North Sea at Great Yarmouth – the Broads.

For the first half of this century the Broads offered probably the best coarse fishing in England. Record pike, specimen rudd and perch, huge bream bags and excellent roach and tench fishing drew anglers from far and wide.

Down but not out

Sadly, Broadland is a vulnerable environment. Silting and the spread of alder woodland (carr) meant that by the beginning of this century many Broads had shrunk considerably. But worse was to come.

In the 1960s, motorboat traffic increased greatly and the wash from fleets of holiday cruisers began to erode banks and hasten silting. Motorboats have also clouded the water to such an extent that plant and insect life have been badly affected.

Since the 1960s, Hickling Broad, Horsey Mere and other Broads along the River Thurne have suffered from the effects of agricultural drainage pumping as well. Because of the pumping, their salt content has risen to provide perfect conditions for a toxic alga called prymnesium. Since the late 1960s, every hot summer has seen outbreaks kill vast numbers of fish.

Having said all this, the Norfolk Broads are still very much worth fishing and with a little guidance you can still find excellent bags and specimens.

▲ *Pike grow big in the open expanses of the Broads, 20lb (9.1kg) fish being common.*

Licensed to fish

Most of the fishing on the Norfolk Broads is free or available on a day-ticket basis. But make sure that you have an Anglian rod licence for each rod you use before wetting a line.

▼ *The Norfolk Broads in summer. When the sun is up and boats are about, fish leave the main rivers for reedbeds and feeder-dykes.*

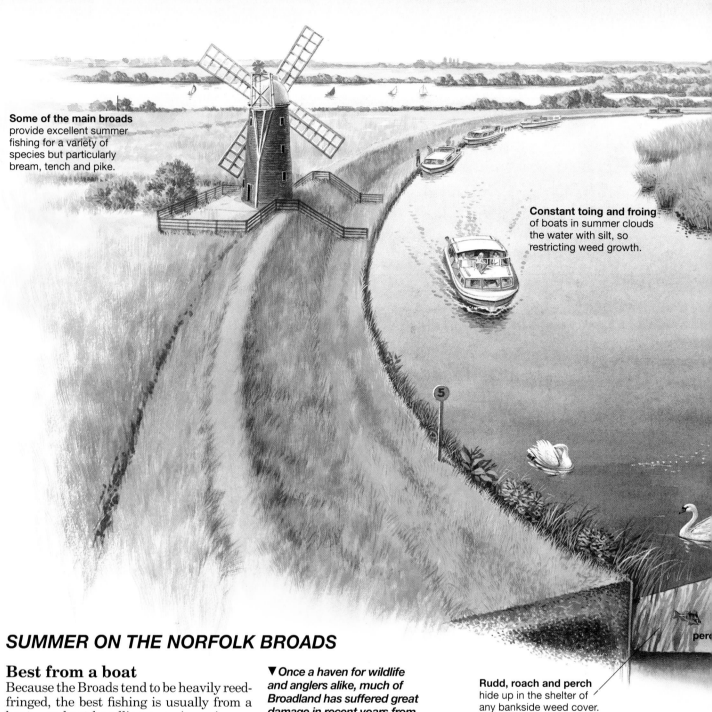

Some of the main broads provide excellent summer fishing for a variety of species but particularly bream, tench and pike.

Constant toing and froing of boats in summer clouds the water with silt, so restricting weed growth.

Rudd, roach and perch hide up in the shelter of any bankside weed cover.

SUMMER ON THE NORFOLK BROADS

Best from a boat

Because the Broads tend to be heavily reed-fringed, the best fishing is usually from a boat – so boat-handling experience is useful. But remember that though fish are plentiful they aren't spread out like currants in a bun. Certain rules of water craft should be followed if you are to contact fish quickly and regularly.

Bream spend much of the daytime in quiet bays and reedbeds, keen to avoid the boat traffic. You often see them rolling or simply basking in the sunshine with their backs proud of the water. On muggy, overcast days you can catch them on bread, worm or maggot provided you moor your boat silently and away from the actual shoal.

Probably your best chance of a big bag, though, is late in the evening and through the hours of darkness as the shoals patrol the deeper boat channels and river courses actively looking for food. But be prepared to take a lot of bait if you want to hold a shoal

▼ *Once a haven for wildlife and anglers alike, much of Broadland has suffered great damage in recent years from growing motorboat traffic.*

Heavy boat traffic makes fishing hard during the day in summer and drives fish into feeder dykes.

rudd

roach

Beds of reeds are likely places to find pike, perch, roach and rudd at the height of summer.

From dusk to dawn when the boat traffic has died down, bream and tench venture out into the main river to browse for food.

tench

bream

rudd

tench

roach

bream

of 100-500 large hungry bream for any length of time! And for the sake of the fish, don't cram them in a keepnet.

Rudd are one fish you can catch during the day. You can spot them in smallish shoals in soft weed, around lilies and moving in and out of the reedbeds. An accurate cast from a distance with slow-sinking breadflake may then take two or three good fish before they spook. Observation is all and it pays to move steadily and stealthily, perhaps watching with binoculars, to find these charming fish.

Tench are the fish of dawn to mid-morning in Broadland. Six to seven pounders (2.7-3.2kg) are there to be caught but location is the key. Look for beds of reedmace then floatfish sweetcorn, bread, maggots, casters

▶ Motorboats are not allowed on the Ormesby Broads and here you can still find the peace and quiet and quality fishing for which the Broads were renowned years ago.

or worms hard against them. Tench and reedmace are always found together because both like a hard lake or river bed.

Pike are perhaps the most famous of all Broadland fish, with twenties (9.1-13.6kg) common and thirties (13.6-18.2kg) always a possibility. True, the piking season is really more autumn and winter but it still pays to have suitable tackle handy in summer if one shows in the swim. One cast then could produce the fish of a lifetime.

Tip Go midweek

If planning only a one or two day visit in summer, try to go midweek to avoid the weekend boat traffic. And to make the most of your short stay, seek up-to-the-minute local advice on where is fishing best.

Where to start

You could spend a lifetime exploring the Broads and not get to know them all. Assuming you have rather less time on your hands, here are some suggestions.

The Ormesby Broads can provide fabulous bream and tench fishing. Little Ormesby, Rollesby, Lily, Great Ormesby and Filby Broads are all connected and together cover over 800 acres. There's no tidal channel into them and they've escaped the invasion of holiday cruisers. Only sailing and angling boats are allowed and here you can find traditional Broadland peace and sport.

The Thurne system has made a rapid recovery from recent attacks of prymnesium. Hickling Broad, Horsey Mere and Heigham Sound total nearly 1000 acres. Together with the River Thurne itself they are beautiful waters that hold vast bream shoals with some very big specimens. Even rudd are making a promising comeback and there's also the chance of immense pike.

▲ Holidaymakers enjoy a dabble from their cruiser. You need a bit more water craft than this, however!

Alderfen is a much smaller, more intimate, Broad. At around 25 acres it's a preserved water that smacks much of original Broadland. So does the fishing. It's a mixed fishery but the bream and tench fishing is famed nationwide, with bream to 9lb (4.1kg) and tench to over 7lb (3.2kg).

Information

Hire fishing boats for the Ormesby Broads from George Alexander (Tel 0493 748746) and for the Thurne system from the Whispering Reeds Boatyard (Tel 069261 314) and the Martham Ferry Boatyard (Tel 0493 740303).

Permits for Alderfen Broad are available from Wroxham Angling Centre (Tel. 0603 782453), whose staff, incidentally, are extremely helpful and expert not just on Alderfen but on all of the Broads.

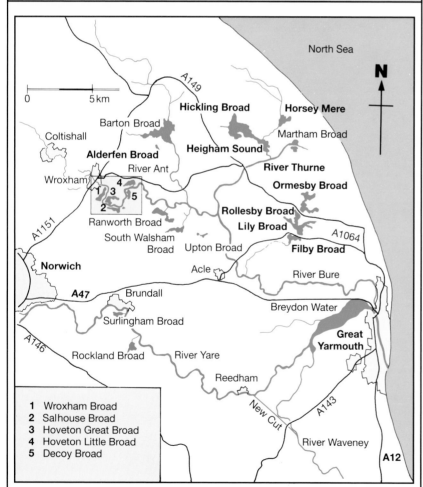

The Norfolk Broads

North Sea

0   5km

N

A149

Hickling Broad

Horsey Mere

Barton Broad

Martham Broad

Coltishall

Heigham Sound

Alderfen Broad

River Ant

Wroxham

River Thurne

4

Ormesby Broad

A1151

1 3 5

2

Rollesby Broad

Lily Broad

A1064

Ranworth Broad

South Walsham Broad

Upton Broad

Filby Broad

Acle

River Bure

Norwich

A47

Brundall

Breydon Water

Surlingham Broad

Great Yarmouth

A146

Rockland Broad

River Yare

Reedham

New Cut

A143

1 Wroxham Broad
2 Salhouse Broad
3 Hoveton Great Broad
4 Hoveton Little Broad
5 Decoy Broad

River Waveney

A12

The Norfolk Broads is a large network of meres, rivers and dykes draining into the North Sea at Great Yarmouth. In summer they are the perfect place for a combined family and fishing holiday. The Norwich Tourist Information Centre (Tel. 0603 666071) can advise you on accommodation. If you want to spend your holiday afloat, cruisers offer both mobility and round-the-clock fishing possibilities – experts in this field are Hoseasons Holidays Ltd (Tel. 0502 501010).

▲ Early morning is the time to track down tench on the Broads in summer. Find a bed of reedmace and the tench won't be far away.

Fishing mill pools

Mill pools – the crossroads of lowland rivers – have resident stocks that are the dream target of anglers.

For more than a thousand years in Britain the force of rivers has been harnessed to drive machinery for grinding corn. Many water mills were recorded in the 11th century Domesday Book, and their sites often remain today.

Few of these buildings are working mills now, although many have been converted into homes. But the water features associated with old mill sites are still fishable and can provide superb sport for anglers.

Mills usually channel a river's current to a wheel which turns and powers the grinding machinery. The water emerges at the end of the process into a deep mill pool which shallows out towards the tail. At the head of the pool the water is fairly turbulent; then the flow slows down and about half way along becomes a steady push.

The flow of water to the machinery was often regulated by sluices upstream of the mill which directed water into an overflow pool that by-passed the buildings to rejoin the river at the tail of the pool.

▲ Bawburgh mill pool, River Yare, Norfolk. An angler, knee-deep in water, fishes the fly in the steady flow just in front of the more turbulent head of the pool.

You'll have to be fairly lucky to catch on the fly – the large mill pool trout are extremely wary.

Tip Mine's a half

Once upon a time the miller's favourite fish supper, eels thrive in mill pools.

Although they aren't everyone's cup of tea, the deep, snag-strewn waters of the pool often hold excellent specimens.

A deadbait anchored near the bottom, just off the main flow, can produce fish of 3lb (1.4kg) or more – especially in the hours of darkness.

A small loach or gudgeon deadbait is what you need to tempt these fish. Half a gudgeon on the hook is not only very attractive to mill eels but is small enough to allow you to detect and hit a bite quickly and so avoid hooking an eel too deeply.

◄ Many mill sites are several hundred years old. The hard-grafting millers are gone now but the mill waters remain for angling action.

Barbel and chub shelter during the day under the deeply undercut bank, coming out at dusk to feed on snails, nymphs and other bottom-living invertebrates.

chub

barbel

roach

trout

bream

pike

perch

eels

eels

Roach inhabit the deeper areas where there is a good push of water.

Prime positions for trout are around the deep white water at the head of the mill pool and in the rather smaller overflow pool.

Bream find security in the very deep water. In flood conditions there are plenty of eddies and slacks to cushion them from the force of the main flow.

Many pike may hang in the slacker water, but some brave the fast water where the dace shoals are abundant.

Most mill pools have a large resident stock of fish species.

Tip *Let it all hang out*

Freelining is a little-practised technique which is perfect for the fast water of mill pools. Put a heavy bait, such as a lobworm or slug, on your hook and then let your line skedaddle.

Drop the bait into the current and allow the flow to peel line from between your fingers.

Specimen potential

In the open river fish roam extensively – they are continually on the move – while in the mill pools large resident stocks of many species occupy various different niches. A mill pool is a concentrated cauldron of fish activity.

Trout If the river contains a stock of wild brown trout, then you'll find many of them around mills. They are attracted by the depth of water, strength of well-oxygenated currents and the wealth of small prey fish. These factors all add up to make a mill pool a perfect haven for wild trout.

If there are trout present, then they are often very large, weighing anything from 3-

10lb (1.4-4.5kg) or even 12lb (5.4kg). They are wise, skilled hunters and your chances of catching them on a fly are remote.

A better bet for trout, if you're allowed, is to drift a minnow, gudgeon or bullhead (miller's thumb) deadbait around the currents, preferably at night or very early in the morning.

Bream If the river holds bream, some of the largest are almost bound to be present in the mill pool. Generally, the shoal hangs in the deep areas just on the edge of the main drive of water.

You don't get large numbers of bream, perhaps between four and a dozen, but individuals can weigh as much as 7-10lb

Dace are drawn to the fast water beneath the mill and also gather where the water shallows up over gravel and sand.

Perch, attracted by large numbers of minnows, loach and bullheads, feed just off the fast water, towards the tail of the mill pool.

▲ *Some mills are picturesque, especially if the water wheel has survived intact. Access for fishing may be limited, though.*

(3.1-4.5kg) – superb fish for a river.

A large piece of breadflake on a size 8 or 10 hook, fished over a bed of mashed bread, is probably the best bait for one of these specimens, especially at dusk or in the first hour or two of darkness.

Feasting fish

The rich food sources of a mill pool guarantee a wide range of fish species.

Perch Mill pools are the favourite haunts of river perch – they too are attracted by the large head of minnows, gudgeon, loach and bullhead that love the quick water over a gravel bottom. They cruise throughout the pool and the overflow, but their favourite feeding ground appears to be just off the fast water towards the tail of the pool.

Here they often chase small fry that skip away from them – you can sometimes see a perch's large spiked dorsal fin cutting the surface in pursuit.

Roach are almost bound to be found in the mill pool. Small ones inhabit the edges but mature fish of ¾-2½lb (0.3-1.1kg), depending on the river, take to deeper areas where there is a good push of water.

There can be as many as 100 roach in such a shoal and the fish rarely leave the food-rich water of the mill pool.

Tip *Put 'em back*

If you manage to land one of the fabulous big wild trout that inhabit mill pools, consider returning it to the water as you would a roach or a pike. They are rare and special fish and deserve a second chance in life.

In January or February many fish drop downstream as far as the slow, deep water just up-river of the next mill. The largest specimens often congregate there towards the back end of the season when they can be caught in numbers by trotting maggots, casters or pieces of breadflake.

Chub and barbel Both these species love

▼ *In this disused water mill the buildings are silent and eerie, but there's lots of life underwater – a fishy metropolis.*

the steady push of water towards the tail of the mill pool.

The gravel holds a great deal of insect life for them and there is a frequent chance of straying minnows.

Along the sides of the mill pool there is often a deeply undercut bank – a feature produced by centuries of strong back eddies eating away at the stones and earth.

The barbel and chub use this as a daytime shelter, only venturing out to feed hard through the hours of darkness.

I'm all right jack

Large and small species alike find what they need in a mill pool. The small fish feast on a rich source of aquatic animal and plant life – and the big predators eat the smaller fish.

Dace flit around feeding on the various small items in the food-rich mill pool. You can catch dace in numbers on trotted maggot or even on fly tackle.

Pike It's hardly surprising this huge head of fish attracts the leading river predator – the pike. Jacks of a few pounds find a rich living on the minnows and gudgeon, while for the bigger fish there is a ready supply of roach, dace and small chub.

With a bit of luck you might find a very large fish at the confluence of the main river and the overflow stream. Here, where there is an area of slightly slacker water, a big pike often sits with dace shoals playing all around. A well presented bait could just bag that greatest of all prizes – a pike of 20lb (9kg) or more.

▲ A mill pool chub – they are particularly fond of minnows during the summer months when they are building themselves up again after spawning.

▶ A netful of mill-caught roach, chub and dace. If you manage to tap into one of the large roach shoals in the pool you could be in for some bumper bags.

▲ Mill pools are superb fisheries in all kinds of weather, in every season of the year, for nearly every species – and with cracking individual specimens. Check out the water a day or two before you go fishing so you can plan your method of attack.

Angling access

Most lowland rivers are dotted with mill pools. But at many converted mills the fishing is private. Ask politely for permission to fish these waters; alternatively, try mill pools open to the public or accessible through angling societies.

Tidal rivers

The tidal sections often produce the best bags and specimens in the whole river system, says tidal river expert Bill Rushmer.

▼ *A view of the Petersham meadows stretch of the semi-tidal Thames from Richmond Hill. This stretch provides excellent fishing less than 30 minutes drive from London's city centre.*

Tidal rivers often have relatively ugly, steep banking to contain the highest tides, while expanses of mud or gravel are exposed at low tide. This, coupled with the need to be mobile as the tide moves, tends to make tidal rivers unpopular with many anglers – but the rewards can be great for those who persevere.

The rewards The tidal sections often produce some of the biggest bags and finest specimens in a river system. The Thames is a good example, producing bream bags to over 120lb (55kg), dace bags in excess of 50lb (23kg), large bags of roach and specimens too – including sea fish. And the Thames is not unique: many other tidal rivers are capable of producing similar catches.

Where to start

Buy a set of tide tables from your local tackle shop. These are essential if your fishing is not to be a hit-or-miss affair – you can use them to find the exact state of the tide at a certain time. Visit the river at all stages of the tide, making notes of any interesting fish-attracting features. Speaking to and observing other anglers in action is a good short-cut to success.

Tides The height and time of the tide change according to the venue and the phases of the moon.

On some waters there are four tides a day. This is the case on the Hampshire Avon and Dorset Stour where the tide comes in, rises to a certain height (first tide), then turns and flows out again. This cycle takes around six hours before starting again on the second tide.

On most tidal rivers the tide occurs only twice a day at roughly 12-hour intervals with a straight tide up and down motion.

Whatever the venue, the tides get slightly later every day so it is possible to choose a tide (high or low) that suits you.

Fish movement The state of the tide affects fish location. As it flows and ebbs the character of each swim changes constantly – slack water on an incoming tide is seldom slack water on an outgoing tide. So don't expect to find species that prefer slack water in exactly the same spot when the tide has changed – look for newly created slack areas. At high tide the fish are often found feeding close to the banks.

Times Most anglers prefer to fish on an out-

TIDAL RIVERS – THE HIGHER REACHES

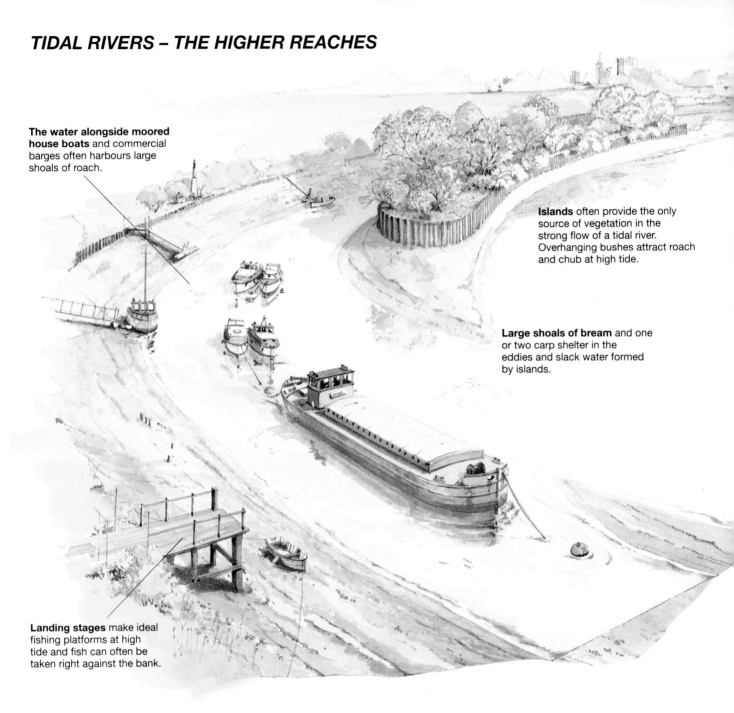

The water alongside moored house boats and commercial barges often harbours large shoals of roach.

Islands often provide the only source of vegetation in the strong flow of a tidal river. Overhanging bushes attract roach and chub at high tide.

Large shoals of bream and one or two carp shelter in the eddies and slack water formed by islands.

Landing stages make ideal fishing platforms at high tide and fish can often be taken right against the bank.

going or low tide because there is less water in the river and the fish are gathered more tightly. There is also less danger of getting swamped. Evening low tides are worth trying because fish often feed when light levels are low.

In general, it is best to avoid incoming tides. The water is dirty – containing suspended silt – and is often so highly coloured that fish cannot see the bait or else lose their appetite completely.

What to look for

Having come to terms with the tidal effects,

◄ Boats are ideal for fishing tidal rivers – you can move up and down on the tide rather than having to move in and out with it when fishing from the bank.

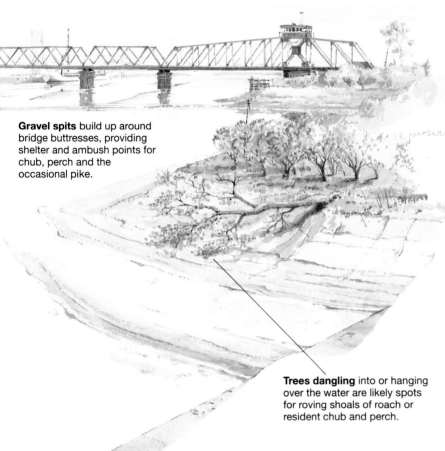

Gravel spits build up around bridge buttresses, providing shelter and ambush points for chub, perch and the occasional pike.

Trees dangling into or hanging over the water are likely spots for roving shoals of roach or resident chub and perch.

Clear gravel runs often contain very large shoals of dace.

▲ *The banks of tidal rivers are usually muddy so you may need to wear waders, but watch your step – it can be slippery. Carry a cloth or old towel to wipe your hands on.*

you can apply the same kind of water craft to tidal rivers that you might do for any large coloured river. However, tidal rivers do have their own distinctive features.

Weed beds are always a good fish-holding feature but are much less common on tidal rivers because tide, current and water opacity do not favour their growth. If they are present they provide good cover and normally contain roach, dace and a few predators.

Moored boats are common in most tidal rivers and often attract roach and – if they run the section – grey mullet. In summer at low water, when the silt has settled, the angler is often faced with clear, bright con-

ditions which roach do not like (they tend to be sensitive to light). Since there is little weed, roach can often be found in fairly high concentrations under boats – especially where there is a steady flow of deepish water. By applying this knowledge an angler can often get a good bag of roach when other anglers fishing the open water are only catching dace.

Islands and bridges Bream prefer sluggish water and are sometimes found in areas of slack water and slowly moving eddies behind islands and bridge buttresses. High, powerful tides or flood water force them to seek shelter in these areas.

Catches vary according to the size of the

The Thames – high tide

On the Thames below Richmond half lock the difference between low and high tide is marked. When the tide starts to come in water levels rise extremely quickly – maybe 30cm (1ft) or more of water every 15 minutes. Remember that it may take two or three journeys to move all your tackle to safety. Give yourself plenty of time – especially if you are fishing right out in the middle of the river.

In general it is safer and more comfortable to follow the river out as the tide flows out.

The Thames – low tide

Tip *A balance of old and new*

You can achieve just the right kind of presentation in tidal rivers by combining modern tackle with traditional baits and techniques.

Heavy, bristle pole floats taking up to 8g are more streamlined than older designs and, used with a heavy Olivette rather than clumsy, bunched shot, provide a deadly, sensitive rig.

venue and area of slack water. Rivers with high tides and large slacks like the Thames have produced bags in excess of 100lb (45kg), often with some nice perch, and there is always the chance of a surprise fish like a big carp. Naturally, pike look into the swims for an easy meal and many of these bream-feeding pike are very big.

To get the best from these areas you really need a boat – it is important to stay in touch with what's going on in your swim. As the tide comes in it may be necessary to move the boat closer to the island or buttress to stay in the slack water.

Marina entrances are not as affected by the tides as other slack water areas, and appear to hold similar stocks but on a more regular basis.

Fast gravel runs tend to be the main dace holding areas. Depending on the venue, you can sometimes find barbel as well – especially if there is any weed cover nearby. Roach like gravel runs too, but on bright days some cover is often crucial.

Trees Fallen trees and overhanging trees offer good cover to such predators as perch and chub.

Salt water penetration In summer this can be a problem – particularly on the lower reaches of a tidal river. High tides combined with low flow rates bring salt water farther upstream and with it come the sea species. On the Thames, flounder and bass are found as far upstream as Teddington (the point at which the river becomes non-tidal). You may be suprised to catch grey mullet too but they are regular visitors to many tidal rivers and can produce excellent sport (they are great fighters on freshwater river tackle).

Tactics

When it comes to selecting tactics, water craft is important on any water but on tidal rivers it is critical.

Strong turbulence and undercurrents

▲ *A power station pumps warm water into the tidal Trent below Cromwell Weir. This encourages fish to feed.*

▼ *Bill Rushmer with a 132lb (60kg) catch of tidal Thames bream – proving the fish are there if you can find them.*

make it difficult to fish with light tackle. This is particularly true of the deeper swims when the tide is moving. In general, it is best to fish slightly heavier than you would on the non-tidal sections – the exception being when fishing for dace in the more gravelly runs.

Traditional methods like trotting bread can often score over the more conventional trotted maggot. Water in tidal rivers is often fairly dirty and turbulent with nasty undercurrents. In these conditions heavy tackle and highly visible baits such as bread work best – especially on such rivers as the Hampshire Avon, the Arun and Adur (both in Sussex), the Dorset Stour, the Thames and the tidal Severn.

Rivers in autumn

River fish shoal tightly in the face of autumn gales, frosts and rain. John Bailey helps you find them.

River fishing in the autumn – broadly speaking, the months of September, October and November – can vary between the electrifying and the disastrous. For autumn is a season of rapid weather changes, from the balmy days of summer to the harsh days of winter, and these changes greatly affect fish, which just hate environmental instability.

Harvest time

The first six weeks or so of autumn, however, are often settled, and when we do enjoy anything like an Indian summer, results can be brilliant. The oppressive heat of high summer has gone but it's still pleasantly warm. Water temperatures are just dropping to a perfect level for sustained feeding and all species of fish are active. The sun is losing a little of its glare and fish feed all day long when there is cloud cover, especially if a very light rain is falling.

Fish somehow know the rich feeding they have enjoyed during the summer is nearing its end. Sensing harsher conditions are on the way, they stock up before the weather deteriorates and food supplies dwindle. This helps to explain the very large catches often made in early autumn. Big bags of bream, roach, chub and barbel can be taken from the same swims they inhabited at the height of summer.

All change

It's important to make the most of this golden fishing, for most years it ends abruptly in the second or third week in October. True autumn weather can set in

▼ *Autumn on the Ouse in Bedfordshire. River fishing at this time of the year can vary from the superb to the downright dreadful.*

▲ *John Bailey fishes a mill pool on the Wensum in late autumn. Anywhere there is slackish water you can find fish – though floating leaves can be a problem.*

Tip **Butt bites**

"When you leger a slack area, use a butt indicator if possible," recommends John Bailey. "You can then fish with your rod tip under the surface, so less debris hits your line, and false bites are fewer."

chub

The **branches** of a fallen tree collect rubbish and deflect the flow, so providing cover for chub.

perch

barbel

Strong winds blow dead leaves and branches into the river.

Falling temperatures kill off summer weed growth.

Dead weeds and other detritus are dislodged by the rain-swollen river.

A TYPICAL AUTUMN RIVER

very rapidly and within days all reminders of summer can vanish.

Cold It's about now you can expect the first frosts, and these have a dramatic impact. Water temperatures begin to drop quickly and this in turn starts to kill off the summer weed growth. At the same time, the leaves of the overhanging trees wither, die and fall into the water. Waterside rushes, reeds and long grasses also blacken and rot, and very shortly the greens and golds of September have all been destroyed.

Windy Frequently this is a time of gales, and these worsen the effect of the frosts. Dead leaves and even branches are ripped off the trees and thrown into the water in

Catching a right shedful of roach...

Big fish specialist John Bailey hasn't fished many matches in his career, but one in particular remains very clear in his memory.

"It was on the River Wey in Surrey in late October, 1976. I caught nothing and the average weight was only a pound or two, yet the winner, who was by an old boathouse, stormed away to land nearly fifty pounds of roach!

"The mooring gave the roach a slack area out of the main flow, while the roofing kept away the worst of the frost. He just couldn't go wrong..."

pike

roach

Pike wait in ambush among the stems of dead weeds away from the main flow.

bream

The best time for fishing is when the level is dropping and the colour fining down after a period of heavy rain.

Fish shoal tightly in sheltered areas out of the main current.

prolonged rain deadens water temperatures, which can easily fall 1-3°C each day in the worst conditions.

If the rain is heavy and lasts for more than 24 hours, the chances are the river rises and begins to colour. As the flow increases, more dead weed and rubbish is dislodged and swept downstream. All in all, this is a dirty process and the fishing does not benefit at all for a while.

Problem follows problem in the latter half of autumn. The leaves and weed that festoon the river make bait presentation very difficult. Floating leaves are a nightmare for good float control as they catch the line and pull the float off course. Even worse is the drifting, sub-surface weed that makes legering just about impossible. Blanket weed especially is a real curse. It breaks up into millions of scraps which stick to the line and clog the rod rings on the retrieve.

To make everything more difficult, the leaves frequently carry a noxious coating that has built up all through the summer from a combination of smoke, exhaust fumes and chemical-tainted rain. As this washes off it forms a cocktail that decidedly puts most species off for a while. Then the leaves rot and this process sours the water and uses up valuable oxygen.

Any port in a storm
After such a tale of woe, you might well wonder if there is any point at all in tackling rivers in late autumn. There is one great advantage, though: the conditions tend to force the fish together into large shoals. If you can find a congregation a massive catch is on the cards.

Places to look are around fallen trees, in

▼ *John Allerton has chosen his swim well here for autumn roach on the Trent. The slower nearside water just screams fish.*

Baiting for the big ones

"Feeding mashed bread and fishing flake on the hook is an excellent way to catch big roach, bream, chub and, surprisingly, barbel," says John Bailey. "Bread is highly visible and has a good smell.

"For specific appeal to chub and barbel, mix small chunks of luncheon meat in with the mashed bread, and fish luncheon meat on the hook.

"Adding pieces of broken up lobworm can also be successful – the smell draws roach, barbel, chub and perch, which you can then tempt with a piece of lobworm, or even a whole lobworm.

"But whatever the bait, don't overfeed. Feed lightly to start, then build the swim gradually, responding to the frequency of the bites and the size of the fish."

vast quantities. Soon the river becomes a huge moving carpet of debris. The gales also help the frosts in bringing water temperatures down rapidly.

And wet Very often the strong winds bring rain, the third main factor to affect the late autumn river. Like the gales and the frosts,

▲ *A pike angler waits patiently for a run on the Lea. Find the roach and bream shoals in autumn and you're sure to find pike too.*

fining down so you can see some 30-60cm (1-2ft) into the water. This is all made perfect if water temperatures have stabilized or are even rising a little. If you can find where the fish are holed up, then you can catch right through the day.

If the river is still high, coloured and cold you must work harder for your fish. In these conditions they usually feed either early or late, and dusk and dawn are the prime times. Your baits have to be tempting and well presented – both always important, but now essential. Your concentration must be hawk-like: a nudge of the quivertip or a dip of the float could be the wind, a leaf... or a very big fish.

▼ *Netting a late autumn chub. All fish feed well when a river has settled following a period of frosts or gales and heavy rain.*

deep, slow bends and in the slack areas of mill pools. In fact, any piece of slackish water is worth a try as bream, roach, barbel and even chub all look to get out of the main flow and into some sort of sanctuary. As the unpleasant conditions continue, more and more of their companions join them and soon the whole fish population of a stretch of river can be grouped in a few very hot spots indeed.

Having found them...
Of course, even when you have found the fish there is no guarantee they will feed. The ideal time for all species is when the river is dropping a little and the colour is

Pike are never very far away

"Late autumn is a very exciting time for the pike angler," says John Bailey.

"Pike know where their prey fish shoal at this time of the year: find a load of roach or bream holed up and you can be pretty certain of finding pike nearby as well.

"The pike might not be sitting right among the shoal of roach or bream, but they are bound to be somewhere close, and with a little searching you should find them lurking within striking distance."

◄ *River sport can be great in the first few weeks of autumn, as the fish stock up for winter. This autumn barbel took luncheon meat.*

Flooded rivers

Anglers are missing out when they ignore the potential of rivers in flood. Big bags and big fish are possible, in both summer and winter, with the right approach.

Most rivers flood, and some do so quite regularly. Flooded rivers often provide an excellent chance of catching some fish, especially larger specimens, yet relatively few anglers fish such waters successfully. This is probably because many anglers do not make any real attempt to maximize their chances during a flood. Therefore they are not rewarded with many bites or fish and simply give up.

Think carefully about where and when to fish in such conditions, or you too may end up believing that the fish don't feed, or at best feed only occasionally and haphazardly.

Which kind of flooding?

Though every flood is different, there are two main types – a winter/spring spate and a summer 'flash' type which occurs after exceptionally heavy rainfall.

A winter flood can be unpredictable, but generally the fishing is poor while the

▲ *The Hampshire Avon at Ibsley during a late winter spate flood. Rivers like this, which are fed by many streams, flood quite often.*

▼ *This angler is fishing in the eddy just downstream, hoping to catch fish that are resting out of the main force of the current.*

river is rising. This is because the extra water is usually cold and it carries dirt which may clog the fishes' gills. Whatever the reason, it puts fish off feeding. While the river is falling, however, fishing can be even better than usual.

Summer floods are almost always good news for the angler, as the extra water is not cold and it brings more food to the fish. As with winter floods, fishing is usually best when water levels begin to fall, particularly for bream, roach and dace.

During a flood, fish must use more energy simply staying still against the flow. To replace this energy they must eat more, both during and after the flood. Obviously enough, hungry fish are easier to catch. Coloured water also makes fish less wary of anglers because visibility is reduced. This lack of visibility also allows you to use larger hooks and heavier line than usual.

When the current is very fast, fish often prefer a bait fished closer to the bottom and more slowly than usual. This means you can load more shot on your line, allowing you to cast further and offer your bait more easily than with lighter tackle.

New swims

A falling river may be best, but it is still possible to catch fish on a river where the level remains high. However, the fish are not where you would normally expect to find them. The flow in the central swims is too fast for most species, so look for the fish in areas which offer protection from strong currents.

The slower water close in to the bank is a good place to start, but if you want to fish the near bank, keep quiet or you'll spook the fish. The inside of a bend is usually slower than the main current and is worth a try. Where the bank sticks out into the current there is often an eddy on the downstream side which acts as a holding ground for big fish. Slack water behind trees and bushes growing on what is usually the bank, and areas downstream of

bridge supports, are also worth trying.

Small feeder streams joining the main river can also be excellent. These small waterways – perhaps only a foot or so deep in normal conditions and usually holding few fish – can become real hot spots when floodwater raises the level to a few feet. When this happens, they offer fish a refuge from which they emerge to hunt for food. The best swims need not be completely slack. Those with a gentle flow of water compared to the main current are also good potential holding areas for fish.

A bank-side ditch that is usually dry can become a little stillwater haven for fish exhausted by the flood current and is often worth trying. Another area of shelter, especially for chub, is a raft of debris caught by any overhanging branches. Dropping a fat slug or big bunch of lobworms under one of these can tempt a greedy specimen. They will also take food that drifts into the raft, so try with floating crust.

The key is to look for any slack areas which offer access to the main flow and the food it carries along. If this isn't bringing you success, remember that sometimes the biggest fish can be caught battling the current in the middle of the flow, though this is only true of fast water species like chub and barbel.

A SUMMER FLOOD

small feeder stream

good fish holding area

Overhanging branches, particularly if there is any debris caught up forming a raft, can be a prime holding area for big chub.

Slack water behind trees may hold big bags of fish.

Before and after

The river Wensum above Norwich, in summer (right) and during a winter flood (far right). The change in levels is quite striking and might throw the angler who is unprepared.

When a river has reached such a high level, it usually pays to wait until it starts dropping again before attempting to fish. However, there are one or two slack swims behind the trees which might offer some chance of success.

If you do choose to fish, make sure you take care not to slip on the bank.

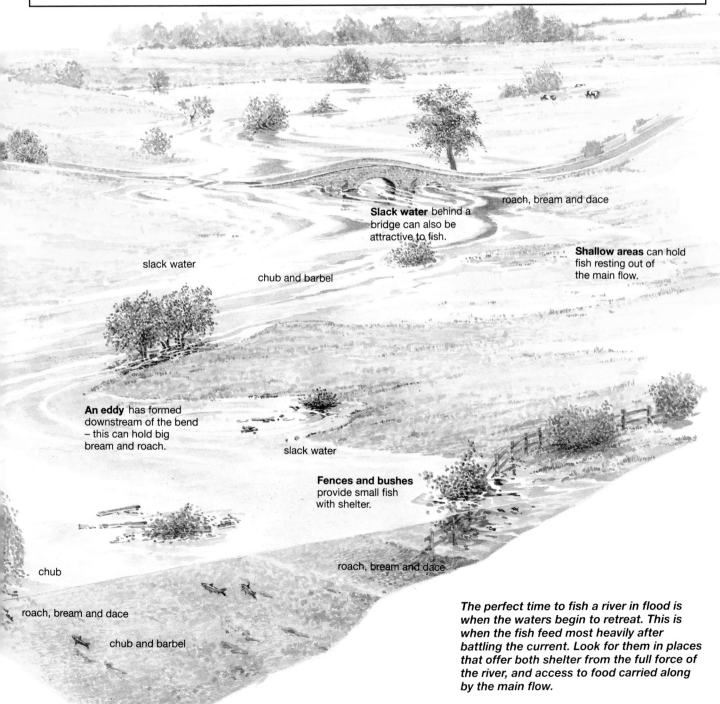

Slack water behind a bridge can also be attractive to fish.

roach, bream and dace

Shallow areas can hold fish resting out of the main flow.

slack water

chub and barbel

An eddy has formed downstream of the bend – this can hold big bream and roach.

slack water

Fences and bushes provide small fish with shelter.

chub

roach, bream and dace

roach, bream and dace

chub and barbel

The perfect time to fish a river in flood is when the waters begin to retreat. This is when the fish feed most heavily after battling the current. Look for them in places that offer both shelter from the full force of the river, and access to food carried along by the main flow.

Feeding the flood

Feeding is one of the most vital yet under-used tools of the coarse angler and it is no less important with rivers in flood. Because of the extra energy needed to stay in one place, fish require a lot of food, but even so it is best to begin with a 'little and often' approach. Fish may still be affected by the change in conditions and too much feed can quickly overfill them.

Coloured rivers can respond well to groundbaiting. The mix and texture of the groundbait obviously depend on depth and flow. Generally however, a cloud-type bait is less effective than a feed that goes straight to the bottom, breaks up and stays there for a while – unless you are surface fishing for bleak or other small fish.

If you want to use groundbait, then make sure you use it properly. It's no good throwing in a ball or two and then settling down to fish. Keep throwing in small samples regularly – just as you would with loose feed. Fish sometimes even respond to the splash of a ball of groundbait. They seem to recognize that the disturbance means a free offering of food.

Loose feed can also be effective in flood conditions. The traditional feeds of maggots and casters can both work well, but in a very murky river casters are less effective. This is probably for the obvious reason that a dark caster is less visible than a pale maggot in the brown coloured water. Worms can also be an excellent loose feed chopped and fed into slack water swims – the juices that worms release seem to drive fish wild. If the water is deep or fast, include them in balls of ground bait, mixed as hard as you need to get it all to the bottom. Alternatively, you can fish the worms with a swimfeeder leger rig.

Hookbaits for floods

Maggot and caster can work well as a hookbait, as can luncheon meat for chub and barbel and bread flake for roach and chub. However, the deadliest bait in a flood is often the humble worm. Worms, along with other natural food animals such as slugs, insects and grubs, are washed into the river in large numbers during a flood and the wise angler – like the fish – will not ignore them.

River sense

You need to take a little bit of extra care when at the side of a flooded river. The banks are treacherous and can crumble after being undercut by a faster than usual current.

Don't wade in these conditions as, in addition to the usual holes and snags in the river bed, the current can be extremely rapid and increases in speed very quickly as you wade from the edge.

▼ *An excellent spot to fish the flooded River Ouse – where a small feeder stream joins it. Sometimes swims like these can yield huge bags of bream, roach, dace and chub.*

Tip Baits for flooded rivers

If you're after big chub or barbel, don't be afraid to put two or three worms on a size 6 hook. In many cases a big bait works best, probably because the fish can get a big meal with a minimum of effort. A large hookbait can be difficult to swallow, even if the fish has a large mouth. It will give a few taps at your rod tip before taking the bait down, so don't strike too early.

Flake can also be a deadly bait on rivers which are losing their colour after a flood, especially for fish which show no interest in other baits. A piece of bread taken from a fresh loaf and squeezed around the hook shank, leaving some fluffy parts around the point, works well for roach and chub. The fluffy bits swell out attractively in the water while the compressed part holds it safely on the hook.

On a river which is very high and contains chub and barbel, a big chunk of luncheon meat can be unbeatable. The cheaper, greasier and smellier the better, as it is this scent that attracts the fish. Since the meat is soft and can break up on casting, use a maggot or piece of grass on the bend of the hook to keep it in place (below).

CHAPTER THREE

FINDING FISH IN CANALS AND DRAINS

Urban canals

Canal expert Vinnie Smith demonstrates that if you know where to look, even the most featureless canals have signs to help you track down the fish. He also explains different ways of feeding the swim.

Imagine you are going to fish a typical urban canal. Often, such a canal is quite daunting, with concrete or brick banks, little or no weed, minimal bankside cover and few (if any) moored boats – an apparently featureless stretch of water of uniform width. To make matters worse it is probably fringed with industrial buildings – warehouses, factories, foundries and wharfs. Where would you find the fish?

Building up a picture However featureless a water may at first appear, there are always natural fish holding areas – safe places with a ready supply of food. By keeping a look out for certain bankside indications and then carefully plumbing a swim, it is possible to build up quite an accurate picture of the fishes' habitat.

On the surface

If you are pleasure fishing and able to choose your swim, you can improve your chances by doing a bit of detective work. Any time you spend strolling along the towpath observing the water is time well spent.

Factory outfalls Industry – so often the angler's worst enemy – can work in your favour. Factories, and especially foundries, pipe uncontaminated warm water used in processing, into canals. Even if the temperature is only slightly higher than the canal water, fish congregate around the pipe. The pipe might be visible or submerged. On a cold winter's day you may be able to see a cloud of steam over the water.

Moored boats During summer boats are too active and tend to disperse the fish but in

▼ *Urban canals often look bleak and uninviting, with few surface features to tell you where the fish are, but don't be put off – it's what's under the water that counts. Urban canals often produce good bags of roach, skimmers, tench and carp.*

▲ *A matchman nets a good fish on the Bridgewater Canal. It fell to long pole tactics – perfect for canal fishing.*

accurate, reliable guide to where the fish are. Not only that, they tell you what's been caught and how. So it's worth keeping an ear open in your local area and checking where most of the fish have been caught.

Underwater
Once you have located a good area, find out what's going on underwater.

Plumbing up Careful plumbing with a fairly heavy plummet shows the contours of the canal bed. A long pole is best since it allows you to lower the plummet and float vertically into the water with minimum disturbance, so you don't get a false reading. By

winter a boat may be moored for several months without being used. It is then that the fish regard it as a roof over their heads.

Find the anglers When you've got nothing at all to go on, bear in mind that the fish are where the food is. Anglers themselves provide a steady supply of food in the form of groundbait and loose feed. It is often the case that a peg is good simply because it gets fished a lot. So keep a lookout for trodden down grass and worn banks.

Litter Strangely enough, an urban canal surrounded by dereliction can be a beautiful place, but like any other setting its beauty is marred by litter. However, it is a sad but true fact that a peg with litter is a well fished one and (therefore) worth a try. If you do find the fish by this method, you needn't broadcast it by leaving the litter behind – take it home with you.

Bridges and wharfs Some features attract anglers more than they do the fish. Bridges, overhangs and old brick buildings reflected in the water create dark, 'fishy' looking areas where an angler can easily see the float. Fish do move into these areas – attracted by the anglers' feed.

Match results Match results provide an

towpath

The ledges are rich in
and tend to attract fis
You'll find they group
top, bottom or in the
of the ledge, but not i
three places at once.

gudgeon, perch and sma

PROFILE OF AN URBAN CANAL

towpath

summer   summer

top of
nearside ledge   top of far
                                             side ledge

In summer, fish
gather on top of the   winter and summer   In winter, fish move
ledges as well as in   into the deeper,
the boat channel.   warmer water of the
                                                      boat channel.

boat channel

Tip Heavy plummet

You can use a much heavier plummet with a long pole than with rod and line because you can lower it gently without scaring the fish. The advantage of using a heavier plummet is that you can feel it touching the bottom and get a very positive and therefore precise reading.

starting a metre (about 3ft) out from your own side, you can work your way across the canal to within 30-40cm (12-16in) of the far bank.

Boat channel A canal with a steady supply of boat traffic has a boat channel – deeper water running roughly down the middle of the canal. On each side there is a shallow ledge. This profile is produced by the boats as they churn up the bottom and push mud, silt (and food) to the sides.

If you've plumbed carefully you should know exactly where the near and far side ledges fall away into the deeper water of the central channel.

Four lines of attack

In summer the fish prefer the undisturbed water around the ledges, away from the boats. Most canals are accessible from one side only – where the towpath is. This is called the 'nearside'. Although there are four distinct areas, it is unlikely the fish are in all four. It is more likely that they are at one depth, somewhere between the top of the ledge and the bottom of the boat channel.

Top of the nearside ledge Depths vary from one canal to another but on the nearside ledge a depth of 45-60cm (18in-2ft) is typical. This is where gudgeon, small roach and perch congregate. It's a good place to

Reflections of bridges, overhangs and old buildings create fishy-looking areas which attract anglers more than fish. The anglers' bait then attracts the fish.

Warm water outfall pipes create natural fish holding areas. Whether the fish are to one side of the pipe or the other depends on which way the canal is pulling.

bigger roach and carp

In winter fish move off the ledges into the deeper water of the boat channel.

Opposite the towpath there is less disturbance – this is where you'll find carp and bigger roach.

roach, skimmers and bigger bream

bigger roach, skimmers and bigger bream

start in a match because it enables you to build a weight with small fish while waiting for the bigger fish to move on to the feed in your other swims.

Nearside of the boat channel You'll find the nearside of the boat channel about 4-5 metres (13-16ft) out. This is where most pleasure anglers fish, so it gets fed regularly. You'd expect to catch roach, small skimmers and the odd bigger bream here.

Far side of the boat channel At about 3-4m (10-13ft) from the far bank, the boat channel slopes up to the far side ledge. This is another spot to pick up roach, skimmers and bigger bream.

On the far side ledge The depth here is likely to be similar to that on the nearside ledge. Being farthest from the towpath it's the least disturbed area. Carp, tench, big roach and bream patrol the ledge so it is worth your attention.

Winter When the temperature drops and the boat traffic stops, the fish move off the ledges and into the warmer, deeper waters of the boat channel.

Attracting the fish

There are two approaches to feeding these kinds of waters – the continuous, little-and-often approach and the 'laying the table' approach.

The continuous approach When fishing the boat channel and the far side ledge in summer, continuous loose fed caster and hemp is a good way of attracting small skimmers, roach and the odd tench or carp. Caster fished just on the bottom, under a light waggler, is a well tested method for taking the better fish.

Although an urban canal may look very different to a weedy rural canal, the fish are similar in their habits. Whatever the water, tench and carp prefer to feed early in the morning and in the evening. So if you are fishing at these times, baits like bread, corn and worms are worth a try – but be prepared to wait a little longer for the bites.

Fish that are topping often aren't feeding, but if bites are scarce try fishing up in the water. Sloppy groundbait and regularly fed loose squatts draw fish from other areas and may get the topping fish feeding on the drop. Gradually introducing a heavier mix brings in the better fish while you continue to catch small ones on the drop. It is an excellent approach to fishing on top of the ledges in summer.

Laying the table A different approach is to put bait down and wait for the fish to move over it. This works well in winter or on cold windy days in summer. There are three ways of doing it – the continental method, the cupful of worm method and the worm and binder method.

The continental method is to 'fill it in'. Put five or six 'cricket balls' of heavily mixed groundbait laced with bloodworm on to the far ledge (in summer) or on the far side of the

boat channel (in winter). It's suprising how often you catch straight after the initial bombardment – they seem to be drawn by the disturbance.

A cup clipped on to the top section of your pole really is the only way to introduce neat bloodworm and joker on to the far ledge. It's very accurate and good when the going's tough – particularly in winter, when fish don't want feed dropping into the swim all the time.

When a binder such as leam (powdered clay) is dampened and added to bloodworm and joker, it makes the bait stick together and enables you to form almost neat balls of bait. These sink quickly and break up on the bottom, so the worm is less likely to be snapped up by small fish on the drop. It's a good method if skimmers are feeding on the bottom.

There's no doubt that bloodworm is superior to any other bait when fish are few and far between, but it needs to be properly presented. A bloodworm that curls up on the hook is unattractive to the fish. If you nip the worm's tail after hooking it, it hangs straight.

▼ *The concrete towpath of an urban canal in summer – ideal training grounds for young anglers to develop their skills.*

Where to fish

NORTH-WEST
● **Bridgewater Canal** from Barton Bridge to Altrincham. Controlled by Northern Anglers. Day tickets on the bank.
● **Trent and Mersey Canal**, Middleport, Stoke-on-Trent. Season tickets from Middleport Working Men's Club.
● **Caldon Canal** through Hanley and Fenton, Stoke-on-Trent. Stoke-on-Trent Angler's Association.

MIDLANDS
● **Trent and Mersey Canal** at Burton. Controlled by Burton Mutual A.A. Day tickets from local tackle shops.

SOUTH-EAST
● **Grand Union Canal**, Mile End, Central London. Day tickets available on bank.
● **Regent's Canal**, Camley Street, near King's Cross Station, Central London. Day tickets on the bank.

Large relief drains

During the 1960s and 70s Leicester 'Likely Lad' Roy Marlow had more than his fair share of success. Here he tells you how to track down the shoals of big drain bream.

Roach, perch, pike, tench, carp, eels, rudd and zander – you can find all these in large land drains – but perhaps the species most sought after by pleasure anglers and matchmen alike is the bream.

The best of luck

Two factors control a match angler's success – the luck of the draw and the angler's ability to make the best of an exceptionally good draw.

Although some people seem to have a knack for putting their hand in the right place when dipping into the draw bag, most are subject to the vagaries of chance, and

pulling a peg with a resident 'shedful' of 4lb (1.8kg) slabs is considered a very rare treat. This is especially true on wide, straight stretches of water such as those found on the Lincolnshire Fens. Here the bream are not evenly dispersed but concentrated in shoals, and these shoals may be several thousands of metres (yards) apart. Drawing on one of them really is a golden opportunity that you'll want to make the most of. But it is surprising how many anglers blow it!

Practice makes perfect, and there is no substitute for preparing yourself by catching a few slabs in a pleasure session as a confidence booster. But how do you find them in the first place?

Law unto themselves

To the inexperienced, these waters seem featureless. Even if you are lucky enough to find any of the traditional fish-holding features you'd expect on other waters they may not be any help.

Overhanging trees or bushes are few and far between, and in any case they won't be a reliable guide when it comes to locating shoals of bream! Likewise, the presence of a weedbed is unlikely to offer much help when it comes to choosing an outstanding swim. Many of these drains have a uniform cross-sectional profile which means that marginal weed may extend for miles. Although such weedbeds provide a safe haven for little roach, perch and skimmer bream hiding from predators – and even for the odd tench, carp or bream – they are not a guide to tracking down the shoals.

There is little if any variation in the width of drains either. Most are ribbons of water, uniformly wide, stretching for mile after mile across a flat landscape – so you can't rely on wide spots.

The picture isn't all doom and gloom, though – there are visible signs if you know what to look for. First, though, it helps to gain an understanding of what goes on under the water.

The simple life

Fish are simple creatures, spending their lives eating and breeding – it's as simple as that – yet anglers often complicate the issue. Bream, in particular, are creatures of habit and for most of the year they don't move very far from a given area. The only times when they really make a positive effort to go anywhere are before and after spawning – and that is only once a year!

Match results are perhaps the most reliable guide to finding the shoals. Many of

◀ The River Witham above Sluice Bridge in Boston, Lincolnshire is similar to many large relief drains. Locals fish the non-tidal Road End stretch for roach and bream. Smelt are taken from the tidal river for pike baits. The cross-section is typical of a drain.

A LARGE LAND RELIEF DRAIN

The observant angler who strolls the banks scanning the water's surface for signs of fish is likely to have the best chance of finding big shoals.

Features such as marginal weed, reeds and lily pads may be few and far between but when they are present they are sure to attract pike, perch and tench.

A slight chop on the water encourages fish to feed - especially when the weather is mild and overcast.

Ravenous dustbin lids

Says Roy: "One day on the Welland I watched three bream out of a shoal of about three hundred fish devouring balls of groundbait full of squatts and casters that had gone too far over on to the far ledge. I crawled along the far bank to see how close they would come. It took very little time for these three fish to suck in the groundbait and return to the shoal. I reckon that I had put the best part of a pint of casters in those six balls.

"Not all shoals feed at the same time - it often depends on the conditions along different parts of a drain."

these large drains are permanently pegged. So if the peg number is given in the match reports you can pin-point the exact spot where the catch was made. Additional information, such as how far across the angler caught them, can also be useful.

A closer look at the match results often reveals that the fish were caught in an area – not just on particular hot pegs. It is these areas that often produce consistently over many weeks – especially during the summer. So what attracts the fish to these areas? The answer is simple: food. Big bream require lots of it and their natural diet consists of pretty well anything that is edible. Even though the food source may

◄ *An angler plays a bream which fell to open-end swimfeeder and quivertip tactics on the River Welland. Warm, windy conditions such as these are ideal for catching big weights.*

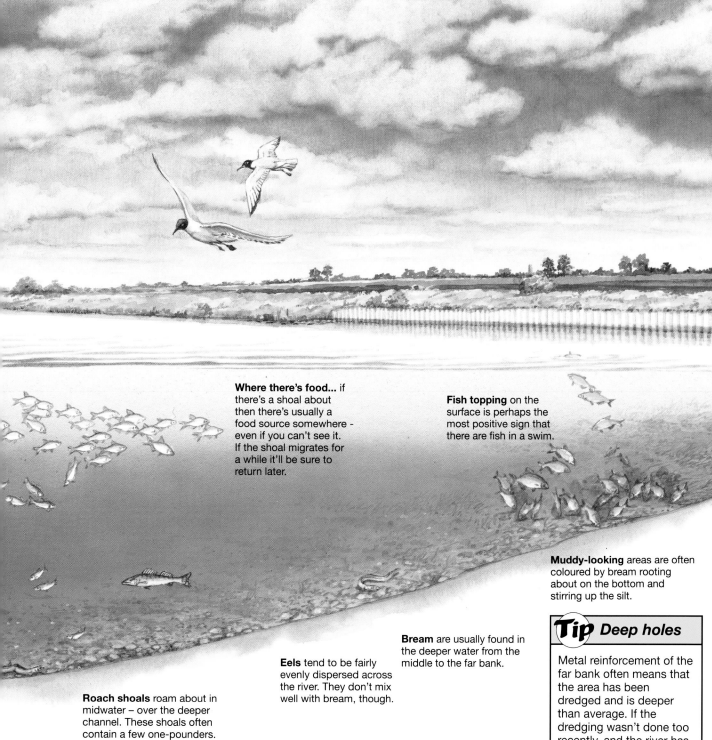

Where there's food... if there's a shoal about then there's usually a food source somewhere - even if you can't see it. If the shoal migrates for a while it'll be sure to return later.

Fish topping on the surface is perhaps the most positive sign that there are fish in a swim.

Muddy-looking areas are often coloured by bream rooting about on the bottom and stirring up the silt.

Bream are usually found in the deeper water from the middle to the far bank.

Eels tend to be fairly evenly dispersed across the river. They don't mix well with bream, though.

Roach shoals roam about in midwater – over the deeper channel. These shoals often contain a few one-pounders.

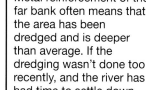 **Deep holes**

Metal reinforcement of the far bank often means that the area has been dredged and is deeper than average. If the dredging wasn't done too recently, and the river has had time to settle down, the deeper water may attract bream.

not be visible to you there'll certainly be one nearby – something that makes the area richer in food than others.

▼ *The north bank of the River Nene above 'Dog in a Doublet' Sluice is noted for its shoals of bream, but there are plenty of pike too.*

Signs of life

It is surprising how many hot-spots have a ditch or other water source nearby. This source is often richer in nutrients – possibly due to agricultural run-off – and this in turn produces more microscopic life such as zooplankton in the main drain. Bloodworm living in the rich soup on the drain bottom, and larger invertebrates – such as shrimps – living in the soft weed (again produced by this extra fertilizer), all attract fish.

Areas where fences meet the water can be good. These are often the spots where ditches and small drains enter the water – sometimes below water level. Underground springs bubbling up through the bed of the drain have a similar effect.

Apart from side drains entering the main

drain there are other indicators.

Coloured areas are often a dead give-away for large shoals of feeding fish. The colour is caused by fish rooting about on the bottom. Large bream (and carp) are often buried nearly up to their gills searching for morsels and it doesn't take many big fish to create a cloud.

Rolling fish are one of the most encouraging signs. You often have to rely on sight rather than sound because big bream enjoy porpoising through the waves and they hardly make a splash. Unless you are looking directly at them you'll miss them. So it pays to scan the water's surface carefully. And be positive – if you don't expect to see anything then you probably won't!

Wind and light levels are factors to consider. The lower Welland, for example, has several bends where the wind may be channelled in a completely different direction. Large fish such as bream feed best when there is a big, warm wind blowing up or down the drain. If you can cope with the wind, and the light levels are not too high, then you may have a field day.

Fish feed well in these conditions because the normally still water is moving – often against the wind. The water contains plenty of dissolved oxygen and is of a more even temperature, speeding up the fishes' metabolism and making them more

inclined to search for dislodged morsels. The extra colour and wash mean that the fish are less likely to see or hear you and this gives them extra confidence to get their heads down and feed.

Given the opposite – a flat bright day – you'll find the fish are lethargic due to the low oxygen content. Their natural food is in hiding and they can see and hear you on the bank. It's going to be hard. It's not magic – it's common sense!

▼ *Many of East Anglia's large drains now hold zander. Preferring low light conditions, they are best fished for during the evening.*

▲ *The Huntspill is often forgotten but this river and King's Sedgemoor Drain are among Somerset's finest.*

Tip Windbreak

Relief drains are usually in desolate, windswept areas. Always take an umbrella. Even if it doesn't rain, a brolly provides shelter from the wind if it is tied down.

Flatlands – fish from fenland drains

Fenland drains can provide great summer sport – provided you know what to look for. Fenland specimen hunter Neville Fickling gives you the low-down on where the fish feed.

▲ *Fens are rich in wildlife, so avoid leaving anything which might harm animals. Litter is a help only to the anti-angling lobby.*

▼ *Dawn and dusk are often the best times to fish drains as the fish betray their presence by bubbling and rolling on the surface.*

 Drain damage

The drains were built to provide more land for farming at the expense of natural marshland with its irreplaceable habitats.

Unfortunately, in many places, removing the water has resulted in massive shrinkage of the peat subsoil. The farmland may not last more than another 20 years, unless some of it is allowed to revert to its natural state.

Fen drains are man-made waterways, built so marshland can be converted to agricultural land, or to help prevent flooding. You'll find such waters in many parts of Britain. The most famous drains are those of the Norfolk and Cambridgeshire Fens, but there are also many in Lincolnshire, South Humberside, Somerset, Kent and Merseyside.

Types of drain

Fen drains can be divided into roughly two types – those which drain by gravity through sluice-gates and those which use diesel or electric pumps to extract the water. The sluice-gate type tends to have a more gradual run-off and is usually tidal, whereas

◀ *There is often very little cover beside a drain. Crouching or sitting while fishing, so as not to make an obvious silhouette, can make all the difference.*

Sluice-gate drains can be very overgrown in summer. Many of them are no longer required for flood control and so aren't disturbed for weed cutting or maintenance. Reeds, weeds and lilies abound.

The fish of the fens

These waterways are famous for two species of fish – bream and pike. Though pike can be caught in summer, they generally feed only erratically. Most anglers wait until autumn before fishing seriously for pike.

Bream live in large shoals which roam the drains in their search for food. Several areas attract these shoals on a regular basis due to the presence of food-holding features. Places where lines of gravel strata cross the drain – and where the bottom can be heavily contoured – hold large numbers of invertebrates. The bream are attracted to this rich food supply. Often these areas can only be found with the help of local anglers or by trial and error.

Another type of hot spot – where electricity pylons cross the water – is much more

those with pumps can flow rapidly at any time. Fortunately, most drains are almost still in summer, making fishing much easier. A fen drain can be anything up to 20 miles long, 100m (109yd) wide and 5m (16½ft) deep, though they are usually shallower than this – sometimes as little as 1m (3¼ft) in depth.

Pumping-station drains are frequently cleared of weed and so tend to be fairly featureless. Fortunately, weed growth is hard to control, especially lilies, and many pumped drains do have some weed.

THE FENS IN SUMMER

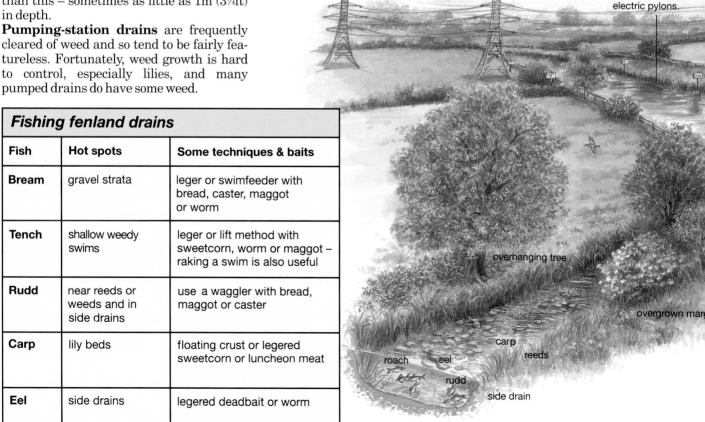

Take care not to fish directly underneath electric pylons.

overhanging tree

overgrown mar...

carp

roach   eel   reeds

rudd

side drain

Fishing fenland drains

Fish	Hot spots	Some techniques & baits
Bream	gravel strata	leger or swimfeeder with bread, caster, maggot or worm
Tench	shallow weedy swims	leger or lift method with sweetcorn, worm or maggot – raking a swim is also useful
Rudd	near reeds or weeds and in side drains	use a waggler with bread, maggot or caster
Carp	lily beds	floating crust or legered sweetcorn or luncheon meat
Eel	side drains	legered deadbait or worm

⚠ **Tempting fate**

While there is very good fishing, particularly for bream, under the electric pylons, there have been too many deaths involving careless anglers. These areas are now signposted, so it is easy to see when you are approaching danger.

Carbon fibre rods are especially good electrical conductors and are therefore more dangerous. You shouldn't use one where there is a chance of touching a live wire.

If you see the bream feeding in one of these areas and you cannot resist the temptation, feed them over to one side and cast to them from a distance away. Make sure you can reach the shoal with no danger of casting into the current-carrying wires themselves.

obvious. There is a certain mystery as to why the pylons should provide a bream hotspot – some people have even suggested that the large electromagnetic field close by is attractive to the fish. A more plausible explanation is that dredgers must work in a more restricted way underneath these extremely dangerous structures and so the bed is rougher and more contoured, much as where gravel strata cross the drain.

Whatever the reason, some huge catches have been made in the vicinity of these features. However, with the deaths of several anglers by electrocution, warning signs have gone up, and wise anglers cast into these areas from some distance away, rather than fish directly underneath them.

The key to finding bream is to look for fish rolling at dawn and dusk, or for areas of coloured water during the morning, where their rooting around has stirred up the mud. It is possible to prebait a swim, but feeding is much more effective as a holding tactic once you've found a shoal. Otherwise it might be days before they explore your section of drain.

Other species

Many fen drains have large stocks of the smaller silver bream. You can catch them in

▲ *This superb bag of bream, roach and perch is typical of a fenland drain, but it requires patience and shrewd observation.*

reeds

reeds

lilies

carp

perch

rudd

roach

roach

main drain

rudd

bream

eel

tench

▲ *Eels are always present in any system of drains, and although most of them are small, there is always the chance of a monster – especially at night.*

▼ *Drains as wide as this fish like lakes in summer. In the absence of any obvious features or fish activity, you should bring them to you with groundbait.*

any area but they are most common in the same sorts of places as their larger bronze relatives. Roach are also common but the catches are usually better in winter.

Tench are popular fish in the summer and some drains provide an ideal habitat for them to grow to 4-5lb (1.8-2.3kg) in weight. Look for them in the shallower weedy swims which are particularly common in sluice-gate and side drains. Again, coloured water is a good sign of tench feeding as are the tiny bubbles which make the water 'fizz'. Some drains also contain stocks of carp. Lily beds are a very good place to start looking for these, though fish rolling or bubbling, especially at dawn or dusk, are the surest signs. A pair of polarized sunglasses is a great help in spotting fish at the surface.

The weedy areas also yield good bags of rudd in the summer, so watch for them feeding at the surface, especially in the evenings. Eels are inevitable in this type of water. They are mainly bootlace eels, but there are some larger fish, with the odd giant of 3-4lb (1.4-1.8kg). They can be caught anywhere, but side drains and weed beds can be very productive.

Although fenland drains have unique features, it is also worth looking for overhanging bushes, or junctions between drains, as these features attract and hold the fish in drains, as in many other types of water.

Top summer fenland drains

● **Great Ouse Relief Channel, Norfolk** The widest of them all, 11 miles long and 100m (109yd) wide. Now back in form after a poor period in the 1970s, with good nets of bream and small fish, it is controlled by King's Lynn AA, with tickets available from local tackle shops.

● **Middle Level Main Drain, Norfolk and Cambridgeshire** Another water that has come back to form, it is not as wide as the Relief Channel but much of it is not heavily fished. It is controlled by King's Lynn and Wisbech AA, and permits are available from local tackle shops.

● **River Delph/Old Bedford, Norfolk and Cambridgeshire** This is 20 miles long with quality bream, roach, tench and even some big carp. It can also fish well for zander in the summer. Permits vary, but Welney AC control much of it and their permits are available from Welney Post Office.

● **Warping Drain, South Humberside** About six miles long, this drain has excellent stocks of tench and bream in particular. It is controlled by Doncaster AA and tickets can be bought from tackle shops in Doncaster and Gainsborough.

● **North Level Drain, Lincolnshire** Around 10 miles long, this drain has a reputation for good catches of bream, with plenty of small fish as well. It is controlled by Tydd Gote AC and permits can be bought from tackle shops in Wisbech.

● **River Crossens, Merseyside** This is a very popular water with good bream and roach fishing. It is under the control of Southport AA and permits can be bought from shops in Southport.

Deep, wide canals

Often fairly featureless, deep, wide canals can be pretty daunting when it comes to finding the fish. England man Mark Downes gives some pointers to help you track them down.

▼ *A typical scene on a deep, wide canal. Appearances can be deceptive – such barren-looking waters can hold surprisingly good stocks of fish. The banks of these canals are usually tinned to protect them against erosion by the wash from large boats and barges.*

When is a canal not a canal? Answer – when it's a ship canal. Nearly all canals were built during the Industrial Revolution for barges and long boats to carry goods from one major industrial area to another. Most are 10-13m (11-14yd) wide and 1-1.5m (3-5ft) deep down the middle – but not all.

Ship canals can be anything from 25-40m (27-44yd) wide, and 3-6m (10-20ft) deep down the centre. They were built to carry goods from coastal docks inland, light coasters being the main traffic. An example is the Gloucester and Sharpness Canal.

The distinction between 'ordinary' canals and ship canals isn't always clear cut. There are many canals the length and breadth of Britain that fit somewhere in between. The Selby Canal in Yorkshire, for example, is bigger than an 'ordinary' canal but smaller than a ship canal.

Here, however, we are concerned with any canal that is deeper than the usual 1-1.5m (3-5ft), and wider than the standard 10-13m (11-14yd).

It's a sad fact that some of these waters are too badly polluted to support fish. On the bright side, some of the polluted ones are being cleaned up and restocked, while there are plenty of others that are established, healthy fisheries.

Canal groundwork

It's essential to do a little preparatory groundwork before you wet a line. The first thing you need to know is what the main species in the canal are. Most deep, wide canals have good heads of roach, but some are also noted for chub, or bream, or both.

The next thing you need to know is where the best stretches are. Read match reports,

Any far bank cover in the form of bushes or weedbeds is likely to shelter a few chub.

chub

roach

skimmers

bream

▼ *This angler is fishing the long pole for roach, but you can be sure there are a few chub lurking under that line of boats on the far bank.*

Look for small roach, skimmers and perch at the bottom of the steep inside shelf.

The deep water of the middle is where you usually find bream, especially along the bottoms of the shelves.

indicate that the fishing is particularly good in that area.

Pinning down the fish

Having found a good stretch of canal, how do you pick a good peg? It all depends on the species of fish you're after.

Roach can be caught from most pegs, though if you are lucky enough to find one with near-bank weed cover this is obviously best. In summer they are mostly found up the sides of the shelves. In winter they tend

sound out tackle dealers and talk to local anglers, and you soon find out where's best to fish. Some might see this as looking for a short cut to success, but when your fishing time is at a premium you don't want to waste it struggling in a bad area.

At the waterside, if you see a row of anglers all bagging up, then it's obviously a good area. If you see a line of people fishing but not catching, it might be a good area on an off day. But be warned, if the anglers in question are fishing near access points it might be that they just couldn't be bothered to walk any farther!

If there's no-one fishing, signs to look for are well-worn swims and, regrettably but inevitably, litter. Again, however, near access points these things don't necessarily

With few if any obvious features, local knowledge is needed on deep, wide canals.

A DEEP, WIDE CANAL IN SUMMER

Deep, wide canals are usually fairly featureless. Bends sometimes hold the most fish but often your best guide to hotspots is match results.

roach

skimmers

bream

Plumb the second shelf carefully, looking for any flat spot. Here you can expect bigger skimmers, roach and sometimes even bream.

to drop down to the deeper, warmer water at the bottom of the shelves.

Chub invariably live in the relatively shallow water right on top of the far-bank shelf. Here they patrol for food falling from overhanging foliage, as far away from towpath and boat traffic disturbance as they can get. Picking a chub peg is not difficult. Any swim with a far bank feature, whether it be an overhanging tree or bush, a weedbed, a jetty or a moored boat, is likely to harbour a few chub.

Bream are more often than not found in the deepest water at the bottom of the shelves, especially the far-bank shelf. At dawn and dusk you might be lucky enough to spot them rolling, otherwise you just have to take pot luck with swim selection. As long as you know you are in the right area, you always have a chance of intercepting a patrolling shoal of slabs.

Tactics from the towpath

Deep, wide canals are no different from other canals in that careful feeding and fine tackle are needed to catch fish.

Roach are, without doubt, the most prolific species in these canals and can be caught on most methods. Two techniques dominate, however: the pole and the straight lead. Whichever you use, fine tackle is an absolute must: 12oz-1lb (0.34-0.45kg) hook-

Try these for size

Mark Downes suggests giving the following deep, wide canals a go.

● **The Gloucester and Sharpness Canal** in Gloucestershire – for bream, roach and chub.

● **The Exeter Canal** in Devon – for bream and roach.

● **The Stainforth and Keadby Canal** and the **New Junction Canal** in Yorkshire – for roach, bream and chub.

lengths and size 20-24 fine-wire hooks.

In summer the pole is best by far. Loose-feed maggot if the roach average 3oz (85g) or more. If the fish are of a somewhat smaller stamp, feeding little and often with light groundbait and pinkies or squatts can be unbeatable.

A pole of between 7-11m (23-36ft) is ideal. By accurate plumbing, try and find a flattish ledge down the near-side shelf. Having found your flat spot, loose feed or groundbait sparingly, building the swim slowly. Once the fish respond you can increase accordingly.

Loose feeding often brings roach up off the bottom, especially in summer. Therefore a light float taking around 0.5g, with no.10 shot spread down the last 1m

▼ *An angler prepares to net a pole-caught roach in a match on the Gloucester and Sharpness Canal. This popular venue is now regularly used for National Championships.*

(3ft) of line, is generally the best choice.

As the temperature drops, so the roach move to the deeper water. The straight lead now takes over. By concentrating on the bottom of the shelves, you can account for some big fish, some of them over 1lb (0.45kg). Light but regular feeding is crucial and patience is now the name of the game – you can't rush roach. You might have to wait up to two hours for your first bite, but catch that first fish and you're on your way.

Chub can be caught in excess of 3lb (1.4kg) from many deep, wide canals. Two methods can score – the waggler and the block-end feeder. The latter is by far the simpler option, as wind and water movement often make far-bank float presentation and feeding difficult. The best bait is nearly always bronze maggots.

Start with a medium sized feeder to lay an initial carpet of feed, then switch to a small feeder after two or three casts, sit back, and wait. It often pays to fish with a longish tail, especially if the water is on the clear side, as the chub can be wary of the feeder.

A 1½lb (0.68kg) hooklength is essential. Chub can bite ferociously and unless you're careful can quite easily snap lighter hook-

Wash out!

"Make sure your keepnet is securely staked out on deep, wide canals," warns Mark. "The wash from large boats and barges can be big and strong enough to uproot a loosely secured net. Nor does it do your fish much good to be rolled over and over in the net each time a boat or barge comes along."

lengths. Also, when hooked they run along the far shelf looking for snags, so you need the power to bully them away.

If conditions are perfect, with no wind and no surface tow, you can try the waggler. However, loose-feeding can be nigh on impossible. It's here that 'Sticky Mag' comes into its own. This powder enables you to form small balls of maggots and catapult them the required distance. (Similar results can be obtained with malted drink powders such as Horlicks.)

Once again, the far ledge is the point of attack, and by fishing a few inches overdepth, with light shotting down the

▲ *A bonny redfin. This is the stamp of roach you can expect from deep, wide canals, but in winter you can hope to catch quite a few bigger ones of around 1lb (0.45kg) as well.*

◄ *An excellent bag of bream from the Exeter Canal. Locating bream is always half the battle when after these fish – keep an eye on local match results as well as on the water!*

line, you can often catch on the drop as well as on the bottom.

Bream respond well to a light, open-end groundbait feeder cast to the bottom of the far ledge. Use a 1-1½lb (0.45-0.68kg) hooklength, a size 20 or 22 hook and small baits like single or double maggot or caster. If fish over 1½lb (0.68kg) are expected, redworms can also be a good bait.

When fishing for bream you have to put in some initial feed, usually four or five tangerine-sized balls of groundbait packed with tasty morsels such as squatts, casters and maybe a few chopped worms. Place the feed accurately in the required spot, and eventually the bream should move in.

Occasionally, where the bottom of the near side ledge is close enough to the towpath, you can catch bream on the long pole. Once again an initial feed is required. Fish a few inches overdepth with a 1-1.5g Olivette rig.

Deep, wide canals are never easy waters, but they are a challenge to any angler and the rewards are there for the taking if you can master the challenge. Give them a go.

Fen drains in winter

Get location and bait presentation spot-on and a Fenland drain in winter can provide heavyweight nets of roach and bream – as well as prime pike fishing – says specimen hunter and angling journalist Dave Phillips.

▼ *Featureless they may be, but on a mild day in winter Fen drains like these can produce large bags of roach and bream.*

Fenland drains in winter are an entirely different prospect from the placid, still fisheries they appear in summer. Gone is the lily-fringed tranquillity of the warmer months. The cold weather angler who is prepared to brave the bleak Fen landscape is more likely to be confronted with a swirling maelstrom of coloured, fast-flowing water.

The Fen drains were excavated centuries ago to drain the low-lying flatlands of eastern England and during the wet weather of winter they do just that – very efficiently indeed.

Most of Fenland is actually below sea level, and during periods of extreme wet

Bonus fish

On Fen drains in winter, exceptionally warm conditions for the time of year can often bring bonus fish on the feed. The odd tench, rudd and eel may well show up and take an interest in your bait.

◄ *An excellent catch of bream is the reward for the angler willing to persevere. Since the fish stay in tight groups in winter you can really bag up once you've found a shoal.*

weather – or the thaw immediately following a heavy snowfall – all the resources of the land-drainage engineers are at full stretch. The Fens in winter are a battleground between nature and human ingenuity – a constant war against water reclaiming what was, until a couple of centuries ago, waterlogged marshland.

Moreover, since the Fen drains are situated in the east of England, the environment can be very hostile in winter. This is especially true when easterly winds blow in off the cold North Sea, coming straight from the Russian Steppes.

But the rewards are there for the hardy angler: catches of roach, bream, pike and zander can then warm the heart of anyone prepared to venture out.

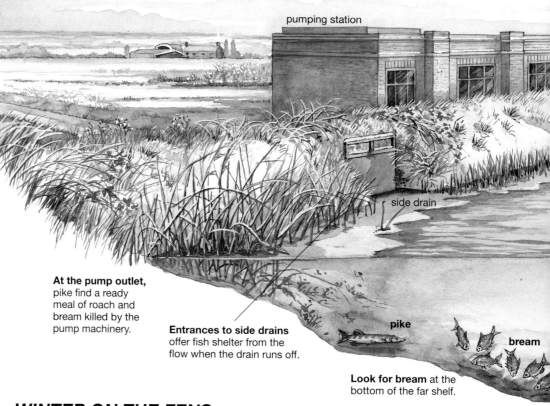

pumping station

At the pump outlet, pike find a ready meal of roach and bream killed by the pump machinery.

side drain

Entrances to side drains offer fish shelter from the flow when the drain runs off.

pike

bream

Look for bream at the bottom of the far shelf.

WINTER ON THE FENS

▼ *There are some really big pike in the Fen drains system – and early winter is an excellent time to go looking for them since they are usually in good condition and feeding well at this time of year.*

Many anglers find a clear day after an overnight frost produces the best fishing.

Winter roach and bream

Shoals of roach and bream are still present and, unless the flatlands are in the grip of severe Arctic conditions, catches can be every bit as good as those enjoyed in summer. Sometimes better, in fact, for the tight, static shoals of winter can provide heavy-weight nets for the angler who has got location and bait presentation spot-on. Mild weather and coloured water can send these fish on feeding frenzies unknown on those hot summer days when the drains are stale and stagnant.

The angler can benefit from the shoaling tendencies of roach and bream. The shoals on almost all venues have clearly defined winter quarters that are well known to local anglers, who are usually only too happy to share their knowledge. Following match reports is another way of finding the best swims. Whereas in the summer the shoals are unpredictable and apt to roam far and wide, the prime winter swims offer very consistent fishing.

These cold-weather hotspots are usually in the same general vicinity as the areas that produce well in the summer. Gravel-bottomed swims and the pegs close to pylons are often good holding areas. So too are the pegs immediately downstream of bridge supports, and the entrances to side drains. These last two hotspots prove especially good in very wet weather when the water is being run off rapidly and the fish require some shelter from the flow.

Bream The resident bream shoals – which in the Fens these days include specimens to 7lb (3.2kg) or more – don't require the same amount of groundbait as in summer. Remember, fish are cold blooded and the rate at which they convert food to energy governed by water temperature – in winter their metabolism slows down so the require less food. So don't pile in the groundbait – a few trial casts with an open-end feeder are sufficient to tell you if a shoal is in residence. If one is, you can usually keep it in your swim by regularly recasting the feeder, relying on its emptied contents

Zander hunt in small packs.

pike

roach

Pike wait in ambush on the sides of the shelves.

Roach and bream shoal tightly.

▼ *A January sunset on Hundred Foot Drain, Welney. Fish like roach and bream seldom show at the surface in winter, except at dusk and dawn during mild spells. But the holding areas are normally very consistent – ask local anglers or follow the match reports to discover the best swims.*

to provide enough feed to keep the shoal interested.

Redworms, red maggots and casters are all good baits, but be prepared to fish as fine as a size 20 hook and a 1lb (0.45kg) hook-length if the bream are finicky.

Roach Winter is when the Fen's roach fishing really comes into its own. Summer anglers can take double-figure weights of roach on hemp and tares in balmy weather,

but it's not until autumn onwards that roach fishing here is at its best.

A small block-end feeder can pick up quality roach when conditions are difficult, but it's the waggler angler and the pole exponent who get the best of the winter roach fishing. Bronze maggots are probably the most consistent bait, fished on or very close to the bottom. Thorough use of the plummet to find a shelf or deep water before any session is invaluable – and be prepared to fish slightly overdepth with the bait hard on the bottom to pick up the better samples. Really big roach are rare in Fen drains but scale-perfect specimens of 1lb (0.45kg) and more are by no means unusual on a good day.

Groundbait is generally a real turn-off for roach. Loosefeeding little and often is a

► *The Cut-off Channel at Hilgay in Norfolk offers prime roach fishing in winter. Bronze maggot is probably the bait to try first – it seems to be the most consistent overall.*

much safer bet to keep bites coming – half a dozen maggots each cast are usually enough to hold a shoal and keep its members searching for more. Only step up the amount when the fish are in a feeding frenzy.

Pike and zander

Winter is also when fishing for the Fen's prime predator – the pike – really peaks. Though artificial lures pick up the occasional decent specimen during the warmer months, after the first autumn frosts livebaits and deadbaits score best.

Those drains in the Great Ouse system that hold zander also produce their very best fish from autumn onwards.

This is hardly surprising. The roach and bream pack tightly into dense shoals when water temperatures fall rapidly after the end of summer, and this concentration of fish in turn triggers the predatory species into activity.

Huge catches of pike to 20lb (9kg) or more and zander exceeding 10lb (4.5kg) can be made by the specialist angler who arrives early and looks for signs of fish activity. Find the prey fish shoals and you can be certain that the predators are not too far away.
Pike can be relied on to feed consistently right through the winter months. They may become lethargic in extreme Arctic conditions, but in general the cold weather sees the best of this species. Many Fen drains fish superbly on the still, clear days following very sharp overnight frosts.

▲ *John Watson with a beautiful double-figure zander – mild, wet weather in winter is the time to seek out this elusive fish.*

Even if you arrive to find the drain frozen over, don't despair – wait an hour or two for the surface ice to start melting and you could be in for a bumper haul.
Zander Sharp frosts and good zander fishing don't generally go together, but this species is almost guaranteed to feed hard in very wet weather. The zander has superb eyesight that allows it to find its prey even in highly coloured water. The mild, wet Februaries we often suffer might be uncomfortable for the angler, but the zander enthusiast knows there is no better time to seek his quarry.

Index

Page numbers in *italics* refer to illustrations

A

Anchor 39, 40, *40*
Ardingly Reservoir 52
Ardleigh Reservoir 52
Artificial flies 64
Arun, River 62, 96
Avon float 60, *60*

B

Bailey, John 37, *37*, 73, 85, 92, *92*, 97, *97*, 98, 99, 100
Barbel 57, 58, 59, 60, *60*, 66, 67, 68, *68*, 69, 70, 71, 76, 77, 78, *78*, 80, 90, 91, 92, 96, 97, 98, 99, 100, *100*, 103, 104
Blenheim Palace lake 27, *27*
Bloodworm 17, *17*, 18, 21, 110, 113
Boat fishing 24, *24*, 25, 39-42, *39-42*, 86, 94
Boatyard 81-4, *81-4*
Boilies 18, 22
Bread 13-14, 21, 22, 26, 42, 46, 54, 63, 67, 72, 80, 83, 87, 91, 96, 99, 102, 104, 116
Bream 11, 12, 14, 16, 17, 19, 21, 29, 32, 33, 39, 40, 41, *41*, 51, 53, 54, 57, 60, 62, 63, *63*, 64, 69, 71, 77, 78, 83, 84, 85, 86, 87, 88, 90, 91, 93, 94, 96, 97, 99, 100, 103, 104, 109, 110, 111, 112, 113, 116, 117, *117*, 118, 119, 120, 121, 122, *122*, 123, *123*, 124, 125, 126
Bridgewater Canal 108, *108*, 110
Broughton, Bruno 50, *50*
Bubbling 12-13, 18, 21, 115, 118
Burrator Reservoir 33, *33*
Bush 16, 59, 118

C

Canal
    deep, wide 119-22, *119-22*
    urban 107-10, *107-10*
Carp 11, 12, 14, 15, 16, 18, 19, 22, 26, 28, 29, 30, 31, 32, *32*, 33, *33*, 34, 40, 41, 44, 47, *47*, 50, 82, 84, 94, 96, 107, 109, 110, 116, 117, 118
Casters 22, 26, 30, 42, 46, 61, 72, 87, 91, 110, 122, 125
Catfish 29, 30, *30*,
Cattle drink 63
Cheese 67, 72, 76, 80
Chub 44, 57, 58, 59, 60, 61, 64, 66, 67, 68, 69, 70, 72, 73, 74, 75, 76, *76*, 77, 78, 80, 82, 84, *84*, 90, 91, 92, *92*, 95, 97, 100, 103, 104, 121, 122
Claydon Lake 29, *29*
Clear water 35, 38, 57-60

Clumber Park Lake 29
College Reservoir 31
Crookes Valley Park 20
Crucian carp 11, 17, 83

D

Dace 44, 57, 58, 59, 67, 68, *68*, 69, 70, 72, 73, 74, 75, 77, 78, 82, 91, 92, 93, 95, 96, 103, 104
Dam 27, 28, 32, 33, *33*, 51
Damflask Reservoir 52
Dane, River 65, *65*
Danson Park 20
Deadbaiting 25, 34, 38, 54, 58, 75, 80, 89, 90, 116, 126
Deep water 15, 16, 17, 23, 24, 27, 29, 34
Denton Reservoir 31
Depth chart 41
Docks, freshwater 43-6, *43-6*
Dorset Stour 69, 80, 93, 96
Dove, River 65, *65*
Drain
    fenland 115-18, *115-18*
    fenland, in winter 123-6, *123-6*
    large relief 111-14, *111-14*
Drifting 38
Drop-off 52

E

Echo-sounder 52
Eel 11, 28, 61, 77, 78, 80, 89, 111, 113, 116, 117, 118
Estate lake 27-30, *27-30*
Exeter Canal 122, *122*

F

Fickling, Neville 115, *115*
Float fishing 14, *14*, 22, 25, 30, 34, 42, 44, 79, 80, 87
Freelining 14, 30, 58, 63, 64, 68, 90
Freshwater shrimp 45, 113
Fruit 64

G

Golden tench 28, *28*, 29
Grand Union Canal 110
Gravel pit 35-8, *35-8*, 50
Grayling 69, 72, 73, 74, 75, 78
Great Ouse 62, 111
Groundbaiting 14, *14*, 18, 22, 63, 64, 104, 108, 110, 118, 122
Gunton Park Lake 29, 30, *30*

H

Hampshire Avon 57, *57*, 60, *60*, 69, 93, 96, 101, *101*
Hemp 22
Highgate Ponds 20
Hook 22, 30, 42, 44, 60, 63, 68, 76, 121, 122, 125
Hotspot 25, 38, 72, 116, 124
Huntspill, River 111, 114, *114*
Hybrid 12

I

Insect life 11, 61, 85, 104
Island 24, 25, 29, 40, 65, 66, 74, 94, 95

J

Jokers 107, 110

K

Kennet, River 57, *57*, 67, 68, *68*, 75, 78, 80
Koi carp 27, *27*

L

Lake 19-30, *19-30*
    estate 27-30, *27-30*
    in winter 23-6, *23-6*
    park 19-22, *19-22*
Laying on 58
Lea, River 80, 100, *100*
Legering 18, 21, *21*, 22, 26, 58, 64, 67, 72, 74, 76, 97, 102, 116
Lift-float technique 12, 116
Line 24, 30, 34, 42, 44, 60, 68, 76, 79, 80, 102, 121, 122, 125
Livebaiting 38, 54, 59, 126
Lobworm 30, 54, 63, 68, 72, 80, 90, 99, 102
London Docks 44, 45, *45*, 46, 46
Loose feeding 21, 42, 46, 60, 76, 104, 108, 110, 121, 125-6
Luncheon meat 60, 72, 76, 80, 99, 100, 104, 116
Lure fishing 26, *26*, 64

M

Maggots 14, 26, 30, 40, *40*, 41, 42, 46, 54, 63, 72, 76, 79, 87, 91, 104, 116, 122, 125, 126
Marina 81-4, *81-4*
Marsden, Graham 15, *15*, 41, *41*, 65, *65*, 69, *69*
Match fishing 30, *30*, 110, 111-12, 121, *121*
Meatballs 18
Metabolism 23
Mill pool 73, 89-92, *89-92*, 100
Mud clouding 12, 42, 113, 114

N

Naseby Reservoir 31
Nene, River 113, *113*
Norfolk Broads 85-8, *85-8*
Nostell Priory Lakes 29

O

Open water 11, 14, 40-1, 54
Orfe 28, *28*, 29
Ouse, River 69, 71, 72, *72*, 97, *97*, 104

P

Park lake 19-22, *19-22*
Paternostering 16, 17
Perch 11, 12, 15, 16, 19, 24-5, *24*, 28, 32, 33, 35, 37, *37*, 38, 44, 50,

50, 51, 54, 57, 58, 59, 61, 67, 69, 70, 71, 73, 78, 82, 84, 85, 86, 91, 95, 96, 98, 111, 117, *117* 120
Pike 11, 16, 19, 21, 22, 24-5, 26, 28, 32, 33, 34, 36, 37, 38, 41, 44, 51, 54, *54*, 57, 58, 59, 61, 64, 67, 69, 70, 72, 73, 74, 75, 77, 78, 79, 82, 83, 84, 85, 86, 87, 88, 90, 92, 96, 99, 100, 111, 113, 115, 123, 124, *124*, 125, 126
Pit 15-18, *15-18*
Plant life 11, 13, 31, 85, 92
Plug 64
Plumbing 15,17, 22, 32, 41, 45, 58, 60, 64, 78, 93, 108-9, 121
Plummer, Dave 57, *57*
Pole fishing 12, 46, 64, 121, 122
Pond 11-14, *11-14*
Prymnesium 85
Punt 39, *39, 40*

Q
Quivertip 46, 60, 66, 72, 76, 84, 100, 117

R
Ragworm 64
Redworm 125
Reeds 25, 26, 28, 29, *29*, 32, *32*, 47, *47*, 71, 87, 116-17
Regent's Canal 110
Relief drains *see* Drain
Reservoir
   in summer 31-4, *31-4*
   in winter 51-4, *51-4*
Ribble, River 69, 72
River
   fast, clear 57-60, *57-60*
   flooded 69, 70, 84, 95, 101-4, *101-4*
   in autumn 97-100, *97-100*
   in summer 65-8, *65-8*
   in winter 73-6, *73-6*
   large, coloured 69-72, *69-72*, 94, 95, 102, 104
   slow lowland 61-4, *61-4*
   small, fast, in winter 73-6, *73-6*
   small, in summer 65-8, *65-8*
   tidal 64, 93-6, *93-6*
Roach 11, 12, 14, 17, 19, *19*, 21, 24, 25, 26, *26*, 32, 35, 37, 41, 44, 51, 53, 54, *54*, 57, 62, 63, 64, *64*, 67, 68, 70, 72, 73, 74, 75, 77, 78, 82, 84, 85, 88, 90, 91, 92, 93, 95, 97, 99, 100, 104, 107, 108, 109, 110, 111, 113, 117, *117*, 118, 120, 121, 122, *122*, 123, 124, 125, 126
Rolling 26, 33, 41, 42, 54, 114, 115, 118
Rolling leger 60, 63, 80
Royalty Fishery 57, *57*, 80
Rudd 11, 12, 13, 14, 21, 28, 30, 32, 33, 34, *34*, 35, 41, 44, 46, *46*, 62, 64, 82, 86, 87, 88, 111, 116, 117, 126

Rushes 17, *17*, 25, 63

S
Safety 18, 41, 43, 77, 95, 104, 117
Severn, River 69, 70, 71, 72, *72*, 77, 77, 80, 96
Shade 11, 45
Shallow water 16, 19, 20, 23, *23*, 25, *25*, 29, 30, 34, 63
Silkweed 64, 77
Sliding float 46
Slug 67, 68, 90, 102, 104
Snag 15, 18, 24, 26, 32, 34, 38, 58, 72, 75
Snow 54
Specimen fish 11, 16, 27, 35, 61, 85, 93
Spinning 24, 25, 54
Staunton Harold Reservoir 31, 52
Still water
   in autumn 47-50, *47-50*,
Stream inlet 32, 59, 102
Suffolk Stour 62, *62*
Surrey Docks 45, *45*
Sussex Ouse 62
Swan mussel 30
Sweetcorn 14, 30, 42, 79, 80, 87, 116
Swimfeeder 34, 38, 46, 58, 60, 67, 70, 72, 76, 77, 79, 112, 116, 122, 124-5
Sywell Reservoir 31, 52

T
Temperature layer 16-17, *17*, 45
Tench 11, 12, 14, 19, 21, 26, 28, 29, 30, 32, 34, 40, 41, 42, *42*, 44, 50, 62, 83, 84, 87, 88, *88*, 107,' 110, 111, 116, 117, 118
Thames, River 69, *69*, 70, 72, 80, *80* , 93, *93*, 95, *95*, 96, *96*
Thermocline 16, 17, *17*
Topping 33, 54
Tree 12, 14, 29, *29*, 58, 59, *59*, 65, 66, 67, 68, 70, 95, 96, 102, 115
Trent, River 69, *69*, 72, 96, 99

Tring Reservoir 31, 52
Trolling 25
Trotting 58, 63, 72, 75, 76, 83, 91, 96
Trout 57, 69, 72, 74, 78, 89, 90

U
Underwater current 37, 96

V
Valve (draw-off) tower 31, *31*, 32, 33, *33*, 51, 53, *53*

W
Waggler 12, 14, 22, 42, 116
Water-lilies 12, 13, *12-13*, 20, 26, 29-30, 50, 62, 87, 118
Water temperature 16-17, 23, 25, 34, 45, 47-9, 97, 98, 99, 100, 124
Watson, John 126, *126*
Weather 33-4, 35-7, 52-4
Weed 11, 12, 13, *13*, 20, 21, 25, 26, 32, 33, 34, 47, 50, 59, 60, 61, 62, 64, 66, 71, 95, 99
Weirpool 66, 67, 68, 72, 75, 77-80, *77-80*
Welland, River 112, *112*, 114
Wensum, River 57, 97, *97*, 103, *103*
Wilson, John 24, 29, *29*
Wilstone Reservoir 54, *54*
Wintersett Reservoir 52, *52*
Wind 21, 26, 30, 35, 36, 48-9, 53, 98-9, 114
Witham, River 111, *111*
Wobbling 25, 48-9
Worm 14, 46, 67, 75, 76, 87, 104
Wye, River 69

Y
Yare, River 89, *89*

Z
Zander 111, 114, *114*, 118, 123, 125, 126, *126*

ACKNOWLEDGEMENTS

Photographs: AA Picture Library 27(b); Adams Picture Library 45(b), 46(t); Heather Angel/Biofotos 14; Aquila 42(b); John Bailey 6, 27(t); 31, 37, 50(t); Bruno Broughton 50(b); J Allan Cash Picture Library 23, 91(b); 111; John Darling 68(b), 74; Eaglemoss (Eric Crichton) 106, (Rodney Coldron) 99, (Andy Freeman) 105, (Neil Holmes) 50(c), 92(t,c), 97(t); 125; (Dennis Linley) 52(b), 64(t), 95(t), (Bill Meadows) 9, 120, (Nick Meers) 69(b), (Martin Norris) 103(l), (Steve Tanner) 60(c), (Bob Taylor) 56, 93, 110, (Shona Wood) 29(b), 30(b), 95(b); Neville Fickling 96(t), 115(b), 118(b); Jens Ploug Hansen 46(b), 117(b), 118(t); Robert Harding Picture Library 20, 43, 85(b), 87, 91(b); D Houghton 49, 54(br); Trevor Housby 10, 13; Bill Howes 34(b); Bob James 3; Dennis Linley 17, 18(b), 19(t), 88(b), 92(b), 124; Graham Marsden 15(t), 18(t), 36, 39, 41, 65, 66, 67, 69(t), 72(t); Mike Millman 33, 114(t), 122(b); Natural Science Photos 16, 19(b), 21, 47(t), 55, 57(r,b) 59, 62, 68(t), 72(b), 75, 78, 80, 83, 97(b), 100(t); Nature Photographers 54(t); NHPA 52(t), 115(t); Janet Oddy 54(bl); Oxford Scientific Films 70(b), 71, 89(b); Dave Plummer 57(tl); M Rouse 113; Bill Rushmer 81(t), 96(b); Kevin Smith 32, 38(b); 60(t), 63(t), 77, 82, 84(b), 100(b); Swift Picture Library 51, 86, 101(t), 126(b); Jim Tyree 15(b), 26(b), 28, 30(t); 47(b), 89(t), 100(c); Alain Urruty 22, 70(t), 108, 112, 121, 123(b); Bruce Vaughan 76(b); Waterways Picture Library 38(t), 45(t), 63(b), 64(b), 69(c), 76(t); 88(t), 107, 119, 123(t); John Watson 85(t), 114(b), 126(t); Ken Whitehead 11, 25, 61, 103(r), 116; John Wilson 24, 26(t), 29(b), 34(t), 35, 40, 42(t), 48, 60(b), 73, 81(b), 94, 102; ZEFA 101(b). **Illustrations:** Graham Allen 58-9; Peter Barrett 82-3, 90-1; Wendy Bramall 124-5; Paul Cookson 70-1; Dave Etchell 98-9, 112-3; Denys Ovenden 12-3, 16-7, 24-5, 28-9, 32-3, 44-5, 78-9, 84-5; John Ridyard 36-7, 48-9. 74-5, 94-5, 102-3, 120-1; Jan Thompson 20-1, 66-7, 108-9; Gill Tomblin 40-1, 62-3, 116-7.